IMPERIALISM

GLOBALISATION, THE STATE AND WAR

D0544726

INTERNATIONAL SOCIALISM 93 ★ SPECIAL ISSUE

IMPERIALISM: GLOBALISATION, THE STATE AND WAR
edited by John Rees

Issue 93 of INTERNATIONAL SOCIALISM, quarterly journal of the
Socialist Workers Party (Britain)
Published December 2001
Copyright © International Socialism
Distribution/subscriptions: International Socialism,
PO Box 82, London E3 3LH
E-mail: isj@swp.org.uk
American distribution: B de Boer, 113 East Center Street, Nutley,
New Jersey 07110
Editorial and production: 020 7538 5821
Sales and subscriptions: 020 7531 9810

ISBN 1 89887 82 7

Printed by BPC Wheatons Ltd, Exeter, England
Typeset by East End Offset, London E3
Cover design by Sherborne Design

A full index for *International Socialism* is available at
www.lpi.org.uk
For details of back copies see the end pages of this book

Subscription rates for one year (four issues) are:

Britain and overseas (surface):	individual	£14 ($30)
	institutional	£25
Air speeded supplement:	North America	£2
	Europe/South America	£2
	elsewhere	£4

IMPERIALISM

GLOBALISATION, THE STATE AND WAR

Contents

INTERNATIONAL SOCIALISM 93 ★ SPECIAL ISSUE

Imperialism: globalisation, the state and war

JOHN REES

The bombing of Afghanistan in October 2001 marked the beginning of the third major war in a decade. The first of these conflicts, the Gulf War of 1991, left 100,000 Iraqi conscripts and civilians dead. The second, the Balkan conflict of 1999, brought war involving the great powers to mainland Europe for the first time since 1945. But the most recent conflict is the most threatening because it is truly global in its consequences. Afghanistan is an impoverished country a little smaller than the state of Texas with little industry, minuscule armed forces and no central government. But, once it became the object of an armed imperial crusade, it stands at the centre of a widening circle of instability.

Two of Afghanistan's bordering states, Pakistan and India, are nuclear powers. Since the bombing of Afghanistan began their dispute over Kashmir has once again resulted in armed clashes. The Saudi ruling elite, the largest single recipient of US foreign aid, is distancing itself from its paymasters in fear of revolt from below. Israel has taken its war against the Palestinians to unprecedented lengths, threatening a general conflict in the Middle East. Such a conflict will become almost inevitable if US government hardliners get their way and the war widens to include a renewed attack on Iraq.

The 1990s saw a new peak for the last century in the annual number of wars—34 in 1992. And in 1994 we saw the highest number of war-related deaths since 1971. Regional and civil wars in Iraq, Somalia, the Balkans, Rwanda, Liberia, Turkey, Chechnya, Angola and Algeria have produced these records and increased the number of refugees by 50 percent during the last ten years.[1] But if we want to understand why our world has become so much more unstable and violent we must examine the longer term economic and political processes that culminated in the wars of the last decade.

Globalisation

The huge extension of international trade, finance and production by multinational corporations is at the core of most people's understanding of the term 'globalisation'. And this meaning does indeed capture an important part of what has been happening to the world economy. But it is worth being more precise about the different pace of development in each of these three areas.

Capitalism has always been an international trading system, and as the system has grown the volume and extent of trade have grown with it. International trade tripled between 1870 and 1913, as Europe and America industrialised. The slump and protectionism in the inter-war period curtailed international trade, but US arms spending and its hegemony of the post Second World War global economy led to renewed growth. The value of world exports grew from $315 billion in 1950 to $3,447 billion in 1990. And post-war trade has been much more a trade in manufactured goods, and much more between industrialised nations, than the earlier period of exchange of manufactured goods from industrialised countries for the raw materials of less developed, peripheral economies.[2]

The growth in international financial transactions has been even more spectacular. The ratio of foreign exchange transactions to world trade was nine to one in 1973. By 1992 it had risen to 90 to one. International bank lending has also grown dramatically. As a proportion of world trade it was 7.8 percent in 1965, but by 1991 it had risen to 104.6 percent. There has also been a massive growth in the market for government debt. This has led to a huge expansion of government bonds held in the hands of 'foreigners'.[3]

International production has been slower to develop than international trade and finance. Much of what is commonly thought to be new about globalisation refers to this process of creating international networks of production by means of foreign direct investment (FDI). The stock of FDI in the world economy increased from $68 billion in 1960 to $1,948 billion in 1992. This marked a percentage increase of FDI in world production from 4.4 percent to 8.4 percent over the same period. But over 90 percent of FDI is concentrated in ten developed countries, and about 66 percent originates in the US, Germany, Britain and Japan.[4]

$\left(1\right)$ $\left(2\right)$

This international extension of the capitalist system has undoubtedly enhanced the power of major multinational corporations. On one estimate, the top 300 transnational corporations account for 70 percent of FDI and 25 percent of the world's capital. The sales of the largest 350 corporations account for one third of the combined gross national product of the advanced capitalist countries.[5] But we should be careful in attributing all the enhanced powers of these corporations to the growth of the world market, as the more economistic accounts of globalisation tend to suggest. There have been some crucial 'political magnifiers' that have enhanced the impression of an unstoppable growth in the power of multinational corporations.

The great cycle of defeats for the working class which began in the mid-1970s are at least as important in explaining the growing power of big business in the last 25 years. These defeats were central in undermining the welfare state consensus that had prevailed among governing elites since the 1950s. This in turn paved the way for the neo-liberal economic orthodoxy that has done so much to facilitate and legitimise globalisation. In particular this process helped transform the notion of the state from one in which government acted as a balance and corrective to market forces into an ideology of government as the handmaiden and advocate of big business. The reality was, of course, that the state remained the closest ally of big business.

And without the fall of the Berlin Wall and the advance of Western-style capitalism in Russia and Eastern Europe, the ideology of globalisation simply would not have had the purchase that it achieved in the last ten years. After all, what would globalisation be if half the industrial world had still been beyond its reach? But the Berlin Wall did fall, and the economies of Eastern Europe suffered the full force of the gale of 'creative destruction'. The triumph of the market was shortlived, its consequences hard felt, and the instability it brought a major factor in the drive to war.

This is why it is important to record the failure of globalisation. The spread of neo-liberal doctrines and the deregulation they promote has led to disastrous economic consequences for much of the globe. The World Bank's figures on poverty give us one important indicator:

These figures, rapidly becoming the most quoted economic figures in the world, show that about one quarter of the world's population is below the lower poverty line ($1 a day) and about half below the upper poverty line ($2). The percentages have declined very slowly in the two poorest regions, South Asia and sub-Saharan Africa, and quite sharply in China and other parts of East Asia, but they have risen sharply in the countries of the former Soviet Union. Over the ten years covered by these estimates the total number of poor people in the world...has either stayed about the same or risen.[6]

These figures do not cover the period in which the South East Asian economies collapsed after the 1997 crash. And neither do they tell us about the growing inequality between rich and poor even in those societies, like China, where industrialisation is lifting the general standard of living. The cumulative effect of this process is to create economic turmoil, social dislocation and political conflict. And in this soil the seeds of war are sown.

The state and globalisation

The role of the state has certainly been significantly altered by globalisation, but it has not been weakened. Even in the area of direct government 'interference' in the economy, the devil supposedly banished by the Reagan-Thatcher years, the facts are at variance with the ideology. From the Savings and Loans rescue by the American Federal Reserve during the last recession to the handouts given to the ailing airline industry in the current recession, there is a lot more 'Keynesianism' around than the free market boosters would like to admit.

Neither have the international and domestic police functions of the state been at all diminished by the growth in international production. To give only one pertinent domestic example, the growth of international production has created, as it must, an international working class and therefore a global labour market. This in turn creates an international migration of labour, just as early industrialisation sucked labour from the land into the mill towns, northern cities and metropolis of 19th century Britain. The attempt to control this process to its own advantage has enormously increased the police powers of the state over immigration and asylum issues.

Internationally the state remains indispensable in underpinning the activities of multinationals. There are no proposals, even from the most hysterical free marketeers, to return to the infancy of the capitalist system, when corporations like the East India Company would employ their own troops. Armed action or the threat of armed action by the state remains the last resort for every capitalist corporation whose markets or production facilities are endangered by international rivals, be they states, other corporations or restive foreign populations unconvinced of the virtues of the free market.

This economic and military relationship with the state is one hallmark of capitalism in the 20th century. And although the fall of the Stalinist states and the privatisation policies of many governments give the impression that this relationship has weakened, this is in fact not the case. It has long been understood, for instance, that the US arms industry's private firms are utterly dependent on the state underwriting their existence.

These, then, are the senses in which the role of the state remains consistent with its past. But globalisation has also set in train some contradictory trends. Crucially, globalisation has accelerated the trend for states to attempt to control the development of the system through international and intergovernmental organisations. The World Trade Organisation, the International Monetary Fund and the World Bank are all US-led institutions designed to shape the global economy. The European Union seeks to make European capital an effective competitor in the world market. And NATO has long been the security arm of Western capital. These and a host of other similar bodies mostly predate the current phase of globalisation, but they have gained renewed prominence because of the growth of the system. None of the institutions can override the authority of the nation-states that compose them. They are as much the site of conflict and paralysis as they are the embryo of 'international government', but they do mark an attempt, particularly by the major states, to co-ordinate a response to the unruly powers unleashed by the growth of market forces. This then is the supranational trend enhanced by globalisation.

In reaction to this process a renewed nationalism is also being fuelled. This can take a number of forms. Those nations impoverished by globalisation and excluded from the elite clubs of the major powers can react by refurbishing a nationalist response. This has been a constant motif in Russian politics and in the politics of the Balkan successor states ever since the collapse of Stalinism, in China, in Iraq, and in Indonesia since the fall of Suharto. Even at the core of the system the fear and insecurity, the sense of powerlessness induced in ordinary people when they are confronted by private and state bureaucracies of international dimensions, find expression in the reactionary nationalism of, for instance, Haider and Berlusconi.

The search for a stable cultural identity in the midst of a changing and unpredictable world also fuels many nationalist movements that seek to break apart current nation-states. Scottish nationalism, Basque separatism and Palestinian nationalism have their more or less muscular, more or less progressive counterparts around the globe. The rise of Islam must also be seen in this context.

The dual process that is working its way through the system was first noticed by Lenin and Bukharin during the First World War. Modern capitalism involves two contradictory drives: the first is the centralisation of capital on a national scale and therefore its ever closer relationship with the state; the second is the internationalisation of the system, the growth of multinationals and international trade. It is the contradiction thrown up by this paradox that, again and again in the last century, had to be resolved by war or revolution.

There is one final response to the process of globalisation and the internationalisation of state power which has the greatest potential to express a real alternative to the global ruling elite—the revolt from below. This revolt stretches from the strikes and protests against privatisation, like the struggle against water privatisation in Bolivia, through the general strikes in Africa, to the near-insurrectionary movements that overthrew Milosevic and Suharto. It is a revolt that is far from homogeneous in methods or aims. Its subjects would not necessarily recognise each other as allies nor agree on strategy or tactics. But for all its variegation, this revolt has gradually taken on an increasingly widespread and self conscious form in the last ten years. The emergence of a global anticapitalist movement since the great Seattle demonstration of 1999 has provided a common language and identified a common enemy in a way that has not been true of any international movement of revolt since the defeat of the last great upturn in struggle in the mid-1970s.

We will return to the prospects for this movement. But now we must look at how the process of globalisation, and the network of state and supra-state institutions, have given rise to war in the last ten years.

The wars of the 'Soviet succession'

The collapse of the Stalinist states in Eastern Europe is one of the greatest political events in the lifetime of anyone born after the Second World War. Events of such great magnitude sometimes paralyse our thought. We simply assume that their consequences are so obvious that we do not need to draw them out. But this is an illusion. The shockwaves from the fall of the Berlin Wall are still reconfiguring the international landscape. The interaction between this crisis in the state system and globalisation is the key to understanding the drive to war in the contemporary capitalist system.

First, let us remind ourselves of the geographical extent of the collapse of the Stalinist Empire. Afghanistan defeated the Russian army in 1989, materially contributing to the decline of the regime. But it was the East European revolutions that sealed the fate of the 'outer empire'. The ensuing crisis in Russia and the fall of Gorbachev then led more or less directly to the collapse of the 'inner empire'. From Latvia, Lithuania and Estonia on the Baltic, through the Ukraine, Georgia, Azerbaijan and Armenia in the Caucasus, to Kazakstan and the Central Asian states, former 'Soviet republics' gained their independence.

It was not clear at first how much of its former empire the remaining Russian state would be able to control. It was obvious that the most westerly parts of Eastern Europe had gone. German unification alone was enough to make sure that Poland, Hungary and what was still then Czechoslovakia would be under Western tutelage. But in the early 1990s the fate of Yugoslavia and the inner empire was by no means so clearly defined.

The break-up of Yugoslavia arose from the determination of the Western powers to dominate the region, to extend NATO into Eastern Europe, and to secure the southern flank of this newly expanded block. The newly unified Germany recognised Croatia and Slovenia, the nearest and most prosperous Balkan state, at a time when even the US was still formally in favour of a unified Yugoslavia. As the break-up of the Yugoslav federation became ever more likely, the Western powers, particularly Britain and the US, courted Serbia as the dominant power. In the Bosnian war Western intervention ensured partition between Serbia and Croatia. The consequent strengthening of Milosevic's Serbia eventually led to opposition from the US and pointed the way to the Kosovo conflict.

The internal relations of the Balkan states themselves, however, do not explain the Balkan War of 1999. If this had been all that was at stake then Milosevic could probably have quite happily continued persecuting 'Albanian terrorists' with the blessing of the Western powers. Long before the Balkan War NATO strategists had been debating transforming the organisation from a 'defensive alliance' into one that could undertake 'out of area operations'. Some two years before the Balkan conflict, for instance, former US Secretary of State Warren Christopher and former Secretary of State for Defence William Perry were arguing that 'the danger to security…is not primarily potential aggression to their collective [NATO] territory, but threats to their collective interests beyond their territory… To deal with such threats alliance members need to have a way to rapidly form military coalitions that can accomplish goals beyond NATO territory'.[7]

In the very same month that the bombing of Serbia began, another longer term Western strategy came to fruition as Poland, Hungary and the Czech Republic became part of NATO. This massive extension of the western military alliance transformed the strategic geography of Eastern Europe. NATO's military border no longer ran between East and West Germany but thousands of miles to the east. It now ran from Poland in the north, down the border between the Czech and Slovak republics, coming to rest on the Balkan states. On the other side of the Balkans lay NATO's southernmost members, Greece and Turkey. The Balkans pierced the newly enlarged NATO frontline at a crucial juncture. For this reason alone, 'stability' was more than an internal Balkan affair as far as the NATO powers were concerned.

President Clinton expressed NATO's war aims clearly enough in an *International Herald Tribune* article at the time. Clinton insisted that to achieve 'lasting stability' in the Balkans, 'the European Union and the United States must do for south eastern Europe what it did for Europe after World War Two and for Central Europe after the Cold War... We can do that by rebuilding struggling economies, encouraging trade and investment, and helping the nations of the region to join NATO and the European Union.' The nations of the area, Clinton continued, were already responding to 'the pull of integration' by sticking with their pro-market reforms and 'supporting NATO's campaign'.[8] Thus globalisation and war go hand in hand.

The new Iron Curtain between Western and Eastern Europe did not exhaust the Balkans' strategic importance for the Western powers. The fate of this region is closely tied to another crucial area of post Cold War instability—the arc of oil states running up from the traditional spheres of Western interest in Iran and Iraq to the Caspian Sea and the newly independent states on Russia's southern rim.

Almost nothing was known about the issue of Caspian oil and gas resources outside the oil industry and some specialist publications when the Balkan War began. Indeed, the then British foreign secretary, Robin Cook, thought that any link between the Balkan War and these resources was so astounding that he took the time to ridicule the idea in the *New Statesman*.[9] But during the course of the war and its aftermath information accumulated that proved the anti-war critics correct and the minister misinformed.

There can now be little doubt of the oil and gas reserves that lie in the Caspian and Central Asian region. For instance, Ahmed Rashid's authoritative account argues:

> *The Caspian represented possibly the last unexplored and unexploited oil-bearing region in the world, and its opening up generated huge excitement amongst international oil companies. Western oil companies have shifted their interest first to Western Siberia in 1991-1992, then to Kazakstan in 1993-1994, Azerbaijan in 1995-1997 and finally Turkmenistan in 1997-1999. Between 1994-1998, 24 companies from 13 countries signed contracts in the Caspian region.*[10]

One careful estimate of the oil reserves in the region records:

> *Most of the oil and gas reserves in the Caspian region have not been developed, and in many areas...remain unexplored. Proven oil reserves for the entire Caspian Sea region...are estimated at 15-29 billion barrels, comparable to those in Western Europe (22 billion barrels) or the North Sea (17 billion barrels).*
>
> *Proven natural gas reserves are even larger...comparable to North*

American reserves. The prospect of potentially huge hydrocarbon reserves is part of the allure of the region... While this is not enough to create another Middle East, the region's possible reserves could yield, if they become proven, a quarter of the Middle East's total proven reserves.[11]

Robin Cook's main objection to seeing a strategic importance for the oil lobby in the Balkan War was that the oilfields of the Caspian were thousands of miles away from the Balkans. But as playwright Harold Pinter responded, 'To get oil from the Caspian Sea into the hands of the West you can't use buckets. You need pipelines, and those pipelines have to be installed and protected'.[12] But Robin Cook need not have taken the word of a vociferous opponent of US imperialism like Pinter. He need only have asked his staff to supply him with the words, spoken only a year before the Balkan War, by US Energy Secretary Bill Richardson:

This is about America's energy security... It is also about preventing strategic inroads by those who don't share our values. We are trying to move these newly independent countries toward the West. We would like to see them reliant on Western commercial and political interests rather than going another way. We've made a substantial political investment in the Caspian, and it's very important to us that the pipeline map and the politics come out right.[13]

Or he might have taken the words, also spoken in 1998, of then Russian president Boris Yeltsin:

We cannot help seeing the uproar stirred up in some Western countries over the energy resources of the Caspian. Some seek to exclude Russia from the game and undermine its interests. The so-called pipeline war is part of this game.[14]

The US government was committed to finding a pipeline route that avoided both Russia and Iran. This point was first demonstrated in practice during the 1999 Balkan War, when plans were advanced for the pipeline from Baku to Ceyhan in Turkey, from where oil would be shipped westward through the southern Mediterranean and Aegean. The completion of the pipeline from Baku to Suspa on the Black Sea, from where oil would move onward through the Bosphorus Straits, made the point a second time. US Secretary of State on Caspian Basin Energy Issues, John Wolf, had announced on 9 July 1999 that the US Trade and Development Office (UTDO) would give between $600,000 to $800,000 for expansion of the Baku-Suspa line. But, as the US analysts Strategic Forecasts report, 'this manoeuvre only completes half the picture':

The US still wants to avoid a confrontation with Turkey about environmental issues in the Straits. Thus, in late June, the UTDO acknowledged that it was exploring other options regarding oil transport in the region, including a proposed Trans-Balkan pipeline from the Bulgarian port of Burgos through Macedonia to the Albanian ports on the Mediterranean. The UTDO said the construction of an additional pipeline out of the region was likely, although it stressed that it was 'firmly committed' to the Baku-Ceyhan pipeline project. As relations between Moscow and Washington continue to deteriorate on a strategic level, and as the situation in Chechnya becomes increasingly unstable on a tactical level, the prospect of eliminating Russia from the oil transport picture becomes more enticing to both the US government and Western oil companies... There is a marked shift to make enlargement of the Baku-Suspa route and a Trans-Balkan pipeline an imperative, and to close this issue once and for all.[15]

And after the war the revival of plans for a Bulgarian-Balkan pipeline made the point a third and definitive time. On 2 June 1999 the US Trade and Development Agency (TDA) awarded:

... a $588,000 grant to the Bulgarian Ministry of Regional Development and Public Works to partially fund a feasibility study on the development of a trans-Balkan pipeline, which will cross Bulgaria, FYR Macedonia and Albania, ultimately linking the oil resources of the Black Sea and Caspian Sea region with Western Europe... 'The competition is fierce to tap energy resources in the Caspian region,' said TDA Director J Joseph Grandmaison. 'Over the last year, TDA has been actively promoting the development of multiple pipelines to connect these vast resources with Western markets. This grant represents a significant step forward for this policy and for US business interests in the Caspian region'.[16]

Since this award was made the consortium involved has given a final completion date for the pipeline as 2005. No such project could have continued without a NATO victory in the Balkan War.

But the Balkan War was about much more than oil—it encouraged the imperial ambitions of the NATO powers in the Caspian region and beyond to Central Asia. There had already been military contacts with the former Soviet republics, but the Balkan War accelerated this process. At the same NATO summit in Washington where Poland, Hungary and the Czech Republic became members there were informal discussions about the formation of a loose alliance of Caspian and Central Asian states. The name of this alliance was GUUAM, after the initials of Georgia, Ukraine, Uzbekistan, Azerbaijan and Moldova. At the same Washington summit Javier Solana, the former defence minister in the Socialist Party government of Spain, secretary general of NATO during the Balkan War, and now European Union foreign policy chief and Middle East envoy, insisted that NATO could not be fully secure without bringing the Caucasus into its security zone.[17]

Even before the Balkan War the US 'Partnership for Peace' programme and Cenbat, the Central Asian peacekeeping battalion, were extending the diplomatic and military reach of the Western powers deep into this new zone of conflict. In one training mission in 1997 US paratroopers from the 82nd Airborne landed in Kazakstan to join operations with local troops after a 23-hour flight from Fort Bragg. NATO advice had already been offered during military manoeuvres by Ukraine, Azerbaijan and Georgia designed to protect the Baku-Suspa oil pipeline.[18] The Strategic Research Development Report 5-96 of the US Centre for Naval Warfare Studies describes the Partnership for Peace as:

> *Activities of…forces that provide dominant battlespace knowledge necessary to shape regional security environments. Multinational exercises, port visits, staff to staff coordination—all designed to increase force inter-operability and access to regional military facilities—along with intelligence and surveillance operations… [So] forward deployed forces are backed up by those which can surge for rapid reinforcement and can be in place in seven to 30 days.*[19]

What was happening was an opening up of the great swathe of the globe dominated by Eastern Europe, Russia, the Caspian and Central Asian states to Western multinationals and military strategists after their long Cold War exclusion. In many ways it marked a reversion to patterns of interstate conflict that predated the rise of the Stalinist states in Eastern Europe and, indeed, even the Russian Revolution. The Balkans were, of course, the arena in which the 'Eastern Question' was fought out in the second half of the 19th century. Then the major powers were fighting for advantage as another old empire, this time the Ottoman Empire, collapsed. Then, as now, the area represented a gateway to the east and the southern Mediterranean.

Part of what lay further east was the Caspian region. 'Do you know how they pronounce Baku in the United States?' the journalist John Reed asked his audience when he spoke in that city at the 1919 People's Congress of the East. 'Oil' was the answer. And indeed the Caspian had long been the site of rivalry between British, Russian, French, Turkish and other imperial interests. It was again in the Second World War when Hitler drove east before running short of fuel and being defeated at Stalingrad. His plan was to take the saving prize of Caspian resources, and then to drive south for the even greater prize of Persia and Iraq.

Afghanistan, the current site of conflict, has a no less inglorious imperial past. Standing as the buffer between India, the jewel in Britain's imperial crown, and Russia's south eastern empire bordering China, and astride the old Silk Road east-west trading route, Afghanistan could not fail to find itself the battleground of empires. The very phrase 'the Great Game', coined to denote this rivalry, was first used here. So it is again today. The Russians are still players, but the British, long gone out of India, return only on the vapour trails of the United States.

There is unfolding across the whole of this region from the Balkans to Afghanistan a 21st century 'Scramble for Africa'. Like the original, there are certainly enough economic motivations to fuel this enterprise—not just oil and gas, but some new markets for other commodities, new arms contracts, new sources of cheap labour. But, also like the original, the scramble for Asia does not solely involve proven economic advantages. Just the prospect, even the unproven prospect, of new materials and markets is enough for corporations and states to want to exclude their competitors. Diplomatic, strategic or military advantage, even where no immediate economic gain is likely, is enough to motivate governments.

In this respect the close links—geographical, economic and political—with the pivotal location of modern imperial rivalry, the Middle East, would be enough to make both the Caspian and Central Asia central to the concerns of the Western powers. The stability of Saudi Arabia and the other Gulf states, still a far greater reservoir of oil than anywhere else, has been a central concern for the imperial powers for more than a century. This is why the Gulf War was the first decisive episode of the new imperialism. But the fate of this area is now bound up with the larger zone of conflict.

Just consider two basic points. The whole debate about oil pipelines in the Caspian, the Balkans and Turkey is driven by the fact the Western states and corporations do not want to export through either Iran or Russia despite the fact that both are favoured by the oil companies because they are cheaper than the options now being developed. And the search for alternative oil and gas reserves and alternative pipelines, the 'multiple pipeline routes' strategy that is now official US policy, is driven by fear of dependence on the Middle East alone. Finally, the course of the war in Afghanistan has demonstrated beyond doubt that the stability of Israel, Saudi Arabia and, perhaps, Egypt rests on the conduct and outcome of that conflict. As US ambassador Nathan Nimitz argued, 'Pax NATO is the only logical regime to maintain security in the traditional sense…[and] must recognise a need for expansion of its stabilising influence in adjacent areas, particularly in south eastern Europe, the Black Sea region (in concert of course with the regional powers…) and in the Arabian/Persian Gulf. The United States must continue to play the major role in this security system'.[20]

United States policy and United States power

A strange thing happened during last year's presidential election in the United States—there was a debate on foreign policy between the candidates, Democrat Al Gore and Republican George W Bush. This was strange for two reasons. Firstly, there aren't usually debates on any issue of substance, especially not foreign policy, between the candidates in US presidential elections. Secondly, very few people noticed.

If we recall this debate now it can begin to tell us a little about the thinking of the American elite, the people who have propelled us all into three major wars in a decade. Essentially, Bush and his team accused the Clinton White House of damaging the military by inadequate defence spending, of involving America in too many overseas commitments, and of pointless attempts at 'nation building' in the Balkans and elsewhere. As Bush's soon-to-be National Security Advisor, Condoleezza Rice, put it, 'We don't need the 82nd Airborne escorting kids to kindergarten'.[21] Gore responded by accusing Bush of 'isolationism'. He defended Clinton's record of 'humanitarian intervention' by insisting that 'nation building' was exactly the task taken on by the US in Germany and Japan after the Second World War—precisely the theme of Clinton's war aims article during the Balkan War, as we have seen.

The course of this debate is uninteresting. But what is interesting is that Bush has completely reverted to his opponents' position within months of becoming president. Military leaders were startled to find Bush submitting Clinton's 2002 defence spending plans to Congress virtually unaltered. Secretary of State Colin Powell rushed to tell the NATO meeting in Brussels in February 2001 that the US would not be pulling back from the Balkans: 'The simple proposition is that we went in together, we will come out together'.[22] Finally, of course, Bush has now committed the US in Afghanistan to a far more extensive and dangerous 'nation building' task than Clinton ever considered.

If we look beyond the posturing of the presidential debate we can see the real physiognomy of the wider ruling elite, which by no means breaks down on party lines. Here we can see some of the real forces, and real divisions, in the policymaking structure of the US, particularly in regard to the area where the current war is being fought.

When the Clinton administration came to power in 1992 its main concern was to promote good relations with post-Stalinist Russia. Concern with the Caspian and Central Asian states was seen as a distraction or, worse, a provocation to Moscow. Clinton's leading Russian adviser and later Deputy Secretary of State, Strobe Talbott, insisted that US support for the Yeltsin regime was a vital bulwark against the return of 'Communism'. The Department of Defence was also keen to secure Russian co-operation over nuclear non-proliferation. Officials avoided criticising Russia's internal policies as part of this 'Russia first' approach.

This approach began to change in the mid-1990s. One important issue was oil:

> By mid-1994, however, the region's energy potential...had begun to attract renewed interest, and the 'Caspian region' enjoyed a remarkable vogue among a small, vocal group of policymakers. By the middle of the decade, there were conferences on the Caspian in Washington almost every week, new institutes were founded to study Central Eurasian history and politics, bilateral business councils created for every country in the region. Cabinet secretaries and members of Congress made numerous visits. In Baku and Tashkent in particular, expectations rose to the point of envisaging special relationships with the Americans comparable to those between the US and Saudi Arabia or Iran under the Shah.[23]

Out of all this a new strategic concept had emerged by the late 1990s—the New Silk Road. Promoted by the recently established Caspian inter-agency group at the National Security Council and a new presidential adviser on Caspian issues, this plan foresaw 'a "corridor" of prosperous, stable and secular states more or less allied with Western interests and providing a balance to what were considered to be Russian, Iranian or Chinese regional ambitions'. In 1998 Congress first introduced a 'Silk Road Strategy Act' to establish multiple pipelines to bring Kazak, Turkmen and Azeri oil and gas to market.[24]

The evolution of this policy was part of a wider shift in the Clinton administration's foreign policy profile led by Secretary of State Madeleine Albright and her mentor Zbigniew Brzezinski. Polish-born Brzezinski is a central figure in the American foreign policy elite, and to follow his career is to see the evolution of a central strand in US policy. Brzezinski was Jimmy Carter's National Security Advisor, and he had considerable influence on the first Clinton administration through his ally and Clinton's National Security Advisor, Anthony Lake. Brzezinski was an early advocate of NATO expansion and, through Lake, was instrumental in getting Clinton to commit himself to this course as early as 1994. Brzezinski's influence continued in Clinton's second administration, when his former pupil at Columbia University, Madeleine Albright, was made Secretary of State. Albright had also worked under Brzezinski in the Carter administration.[25]

Brzezinski's 'three grand imperatives of imperial geostrategy' are 'to prevent collusion and maintain security among the vassals, to keep tributaries pliant and protected, and to keep the barbarians from coming together'. And the most pressing task is to 'consolidate and perpetuate the prevailing geopolitical pluralism on the map of Eurasia' by 'manoeuvre and manipulation in order to prevent the emergence of a hostile coalition that could eventually seek to challenge America's primacy'. Those that must be divided and ruled are Germany, Russia, China, Iran and Japan.[26]

It was Brzezinski who infamously defended US support for the Taliban thus: 'What is more important in the world view of history? The Taliban or the fall of the Soviet Empire? A few stirred-up Muslims or the liberation of Central Europe and the end of the Cold War?'[27] And once this task was performed, and NATO expansion achieved, Brzezinski became a firm advocate of war in the Balkans. This was in part because he saw the Balkan War as a testing ground for US policy throughout the whole Caspian and Central Asian area: 'In the Brzezinski scheme of things…"Serbia" is Russia, and Croatia, Bosnia, Kosovo, etc, are the Ukraine, the Baltic states, Georgia and the former Soviet republics of "the Eurasian Balkans".'[28] And, of course:

> …having become an advocate for American oil companies wishing to estab-
> lish themselves in the former Soviet republics of the Caucasus and Central
> Asia, Brzezinski regards American predominance in this region…as a prime
> objective. With this in mind, apart from alliances with China and Turkey, our
> champion of democracy takes a positive view both of the strengthening of
> relations between Pakistan and Afghanistan (with the Taliban acting as
> cement) and of the Islamic resurgence in Saudi Arabia as well as Iran (with
> which he favours an alliance).[29]

It does not take great perspicacity to see in this scenario the outlines of US diplomacy in the Afghan conflict, notwithstanding the small alteration that the 'few stirred-up Muslims' are giving the US elite more trouble than Brzezinski foresaw.

The Brzezinski strategy has not gone unopposed among America's rulers. Some, like Clinton's Secretary of State Warren Christopher, were ambivalent about NATO expansion. Some have seen Islam as a threat rather than a useful counter in the game of geopolitical *realpolitik*. Some, like Strobe Talbott, started out the 1990s with a more benign and inclusive attitude toward Russia, hoping that it could be brought into the Western camp as more of an ally than a competitor. But a combination of the catastrophic performance of the Russian and former Soviet republics' economies, deeply authoritarian governments throughout the region, and the logic of two wars in three years have given the 'expansionists' ascendancy.

The Bush cabinet itself is a remarkable group of people. Vice-president Dick Cheney is an oil executive and the former Secretary of Defence. Condoleezza Rice is the director of a transnational oil corporation and a

Russian scholar. Secretary of State Colin Powell has no diplomatic training but was, of course, chair of the Joint Chiefs of Staff during the Gulf War. Donald Rumsfeld, Secretary of Defence, is a former chief executive officer of Searle Pharmaceuticals and was, with Dick Cheney, the featured speaker at the Russian-American Business Leaders Forum in May 2000. Rumsfeld and his deputy, Paul Wolfowitz, argued passionately for action to overthrow Saddam Hussein in the late 1990s. It is safe to say that the central concerns of this group are oil, Russia and the military.

In any case, the real barrier to the 'expansionists' lies less in the internal divisions in the American ruling class and more in the limits of American power. And, for all that US power seems unassailable, the truth is that it has very real limitations.

The basic paradox underlying the US imperial project at the beginning of the 21st century is this—it has military capability beyond the reach of most of its competitors, but it does not have the economic capability to rebuild a world economy repeatedly suffering recession and slow growth at its core, and devastation in much of its periphery. This contrasts with the highpoint of American hegemony in the immediate post Second World War period. Then the proportion of American economic power in the world economy as a whole was much greater, underpinning its political and military reconstruction of Europe, and its inheritance of responsibility for those areas of the world left behind by the retreat of European colonialism.[30] Then arms spending by America could sustain the longest boom in the history of capitalism. Now, however much it may assist the US economy in the short term, arms spending is not capable of once more lifting the world economy into a period of expansion in which growth rates are once again double the current average for the industrialised economies.

This economic context has profound relevance to the fate of the Eurasian zone of conflict that we have been examining. Globalisation and the opening up of the Russian sphere of influence have ensured an economic and military rush into this area by the US and other Western powers. But the economic aspect of this has certainly been no new Marshall Plan capable of bringing the prosperity that so many assumed would follow the collapse of Stalinism. The Russian economy itself underwent a disastrous crisis in the 1990s, deepened by the South East Asian crash in 1997. In the former Soviet republics much investment has been promised but relatively little has been delivered, especially if we exclude oil and gas related resources. And in the period 1997-1999 Central Eurasia's trade with the rest of the world declined by 40 percent. The consequence is that since 1997 life expectancy, literacy, and fertility and nutrition levels have fallen in nearly every country in the region. Population growth in Kyrgyzstan fell by 31 percent in 1999, in Armenia by 25 percent in 1998, and in Afghanistan by an average of 15 percent a year.[31]

All this is a long way from the 'prosperous corridor' dreamt of by the best and the brightest at the NSC in the mid-1990s. Now the US and the other major powers have a darker vision of their purpose in the region. As the 1990s progressed, they were inclined to see it as an extension of Afghanistan—described by one Indian expert as 'the perpetual vortex of a storm that spews forth all manner of evil'.[32] Conveniently forgetting their own part in creating this storm, 'all the major powers with interests in Central Eurasia regard maintaining stability there as the most important issue'.[33]

So where globalisation has failed, the military must step in. This is the pattern time and again in relation to the oil pipelines. The Baku-Ceyhan pipeline was delayed for a long period by the Turkish state's inability to deal with the Kurdish revolt. The Baku-Suspa route was imperilled by Chechen separatists who, on one occasion, blew up an existing pipeline. The Bulgaria-Albania pipeline was impossible until NATO's victory in the Balkans. The Afghan civil war eventually forced the cancellation of the Unacol pipeline from Tajikistan to Pakistan through Afghanistan. Thus geopolitical strategy both contradict and mutually reinforce each other.

Russia, China and the new imperialism

The major powers agree on the 'need for stability', but they do not agree on how this is to be achieved. One critical relationship, that between the US and Russia, has inevitably been worsened by the 'expansionist' policy that now guides America. Vladimir Putin may welcome the licence that the 'war against terrorism' gives him to pursue the war in Chechnya. He may even gain more leverage in the bargaining over the abandonment of the Anti Ballistic Missile Treaty because the US needs his support for operations in Afghanistan. But the fundamental direction of Russian foreign policy since the late 1990s, and especially since the Balkan War, has been to become more assertive of its interests in the 'near abroad'.

The change began with the 'Primakov doctrine', named after Russia's foreign minister from 1996 to 1998, which called for a strengthening of opposition to the influence of 'outsiders' in Russia's 'near abroad'. But it was in the late 1990s that this became a more serious approach. Russia released a new defence doctrine calling for stronger defence arrangements with the former Soviet states and a major increase in defence spending. At the January 2000 Confederation of Independent States summit Putin proposed, and for the first time the other CIS leaders accepted, a greater Russian role in co-ordinating defence 'against terrorism'. Thus Putin's coalition preceded Bush's by more than a year and a half. Putin will be well aware that closer co-operation with the Soviet successor states over 'terrorism' can lead to greater co-operation in resisting US and NATO expansionism.

China has its own interests in 'maintaining stability' in its border province with Afghanistan. On the broader canvas it is the subject of overtures from both Russia and the US. The US, for instance, is both trying to assist China's passage into the World Trade Organisation and override China's objections to its 'theatre missile defence' strategy. China, in response, has been advocating the doctrine of a 'multi-polar' world designed to limit unilateral action by the US, undermine its commitment to the deployment of forces in the region, and unsettle those countries that host US bases. This approach was the subject of a joint Chinese-Russian communique when President Jiang Zemin visited Moscow in November 1999.

A Sino-Russian alliance is one development the US fears most, as Brzezinski made clear. There have been signs that some such understanding may develop, despite the fact that neither China nor Russia can, for the moment, afford to completely alienate the US. In the last five years a new regional organisation has been built up—the Shanghai Group. Its members are China, Russia, Kazakstan, Kyrgyzstan and Tajikistan. The group co-operates on a range of trade, cultural, security and military affairs. The alliance has resulted in the sale of Russian C-30 fighters to China. And, of course, China and Russia are both opposed to US plans for missile defence.

Other lesser powers—Pakistan is the obvious current example—negotiate the treacherous waters between pleasing the major powers and sustaining their own interests.

This picture illustrates two fundamental aspects of the new imperialism that I recorded at its birth. The first is that the new imperialism is much more complex and unstable than the old bi-polar world of the Cold War:

> ...the central feature of the new imperialism is that even the greatest of the great powers is no longer so great that it has the same capacity to structure the world, or even particular regions of the world, that the two superpowers had at the height of the Cold War. They now try to control a less stable world while still competing with each other. Sometimes they will achieve this through mutual but unstable agreement, sometimes through economic competition, sometimes by war or the threat of war, and most often through a combination of all of these... It [is] precisely in the combined and uneven competition that the instability of the system rest[s].[34]

Secondly, the new fractured 'multi-polar' world inhibits the US from being able to act alone. As the Gulf War showed:

> *International co-ordination is not just a question of cloaking US power in multilateral clothes. The US found such multinational co-ordination **necessary** as well as **desirable**. Unilateral military action against Iraq was too dangerous and unilateral economic action was impossible. So the need for international action speaks of US weakness, not strength.*[35]

These characteristics of the system have become more pronounced in the two major wars since the Gulf War. In the Afghan war the degree of bribery necessary to form an international 'coalition' reached epidemic proportions.

Pakistan was a 'rogue state' before the Afghan war because it fought a war with India over Kashmir and continued testing nuclear weapons, and because General Musharraf came to power in a military coup. Now the sanctions imposed are being lifted, debt is being rescheduled, aid and loans offered, and renewed fighting in Kashmir ignored by the US. In short, a new rogue state, much more dangerous than Afghanistan, is being created before our eyes.

The last, bloody edition of Russia's war against Chechnya was conducted after NATO's attack on the Balkans. This fact, as the Russian government clearly appreciated, nullified Western criticism. Now George Bush has given Putin's 'war on terrorism' legitimacy. But US troop deployment in Uzbekistan, where the government already looks to reviving its pipeline projects with US oil companies, and other Central Asian states is sowing the seeds of future conflicts. China, the second great long term imperial competitor for the US, has won a partial lifting of sanctions on the sale of military equipment. These were first imposed after the Tiananmen Square massacre in 1989.[36]

In the Middle East the bribery involves increased instability at every turn. The 'war against terrorism' has unleashed the Israeli state's armed forces on the Palestinians, inflamed Arab opinion and called into question the stability of pro-US governments in the region. In response the US is selling rockets to Egypt, even greater numbers of fighters and missiles to Oman, and has allowed Syria a place on the UN Security Council. There has even been a purely verbal US commitment to a Palestinian state. The arms will stay in the Middle East—the promise of a Palestinian state will not. Cynicism and anger about the 'peace process' will deepen as yet another imperial promise is broken.

America was created as a modern nation by white settlers who offered the native population of that continent weapons and commodities in return for the destruction of their society. More than three centuries later the seeds of future wars are being sown by the US government's need to ply an unwilling world with arms and money in order to sustain its imperial dominance.

The left and imperialism

The fall of Stalinism has had a profound effect on the left. For the duration of the Cold War imperial rivalry was, by definition, a bi-polar affair. This was true despite the fact that the actual conflicts were mostly fought in the Third World, sometimes by proxy. The collapse of the USSR, which so many identified with socialism, led to a widespread pessimism on the left. For many it seemed as if the US was now the unchallenged ruler of the globe, no longer subject to challenge by other powers. A host of theorists have come forward to testify to this untrammelled power.

The trend began early in the 1990s with the popularisation of Francis Fukuyama's thesis that the fall of Stalinism meant that there were no longer any serious challenges to the liberal democratic, free market model embodied by the US. The corollary was that no two states so constituted would ever fight a war. The common or garden version of this idea is that 'no two states with a McDonald's have ever gone to war'. In other more left wing accounts the US appears as an all-powerful 'hegemon', whose actions are accounted for simply in terms of its ability to oblige its allies and enemies to do its bidding. These accounts have a familiar feel because they reproduce some of the arguments first advanced by Karl Kautsky, the theoretician of the Second International.

Kautsky argued that the capitalist system in the early 20th century had entered an 'ultra-imperialist' era. The key characteristic of ultra-imperialism was that conflict between the major powers was now impossible because capitalist firms had become so large, and the economies of the major capitalist powers so integrated, that conflict between them would be too damaging to contemplate. Kautsky foresaw 'a federation of the strongest imperial powers who renounce their arms race' and therefore 'the threat to world peace'. Modern accounts of the monolithic power of the US reach a similar conclusion. There may be 'colonial' wars, but no general conflict can result from them because the power of the US is so overwhelming.

There is of course a grain of truth in this argument. US military capacity is the greatest in the world. And the US economy has boomed in the 1990s while some of its post Cold War competitors have, like Japan, faltered. But what Kautsky ignored, and what the modern advocates of monolithic imperialism ignore, is that the imperialist system remains the site of conflict between the major powers. The US does have by far the greatest military arsenal in the world, but its ability to underwrite the economic stability of the system has declined greatly in the post-war period. And the social and political instability that results from this fact constantly throws up challenges to US power.

These challenges rarely begin with conflicts between major powers. More typically they involve, as they have done throughout the history of imperialism, minor powers—'rogue states' in the modern parlance. But confrontations between the imperialist states and smaller nations frequently come to involve rivalries between the imperialist states themselves. The relative economic decline of the US, plus the fact that even militarily it is powerful but not all-powerful, means that the troubled business of coalition building is unavoidable. Equally unavoidable is the fact, greatly feared by US strategists, that other nations may build coalitions against the US. A succession of 'colonial' conflicts may be necessary before such divisions between the major powers threaten a major war—but the root causes of such a conflict exist in the new imperialism.

This situation is strongly reminiscent of the unstable and shifting alliances characteristic of the imperialist system before the Cold War. Then too there was a dominant power, Britain. But this did not prevent either colonial wars or the eventual emergence of the conditions for a war between the major powers. Indeed, it is arguable that the rivalries inherent in the modern world order make imperialism a much more war-prone system that the fearful stability of the bi-polar Cold War.

The fall of Stalinism has also had a second and equally profound effect on the left's thinking. This concerns the struggle against imperialism. From the time of the degeneration of the Russian Revolution in the late 1920s much of the left internationally identified socialism with state control of the economy, no matter how authoritarian and undemocratic the regime. This identification was made significantly greater when the Stalinist model was extended to Eastern Europe, China, Cuba and a variety of other post-colonial regimes after the Second World War. For the Communist parties and their fellow travellers, including many in social democratic parties, this meant that regimes which found themselves in opposition to imperialism also had 'progressive' social structures. Cuba or North Vietnam, for instance, were not only to be supported because they had the right to national self determination, but also because they were in some way inherently progressive, even socialist.

The fall of Stalinism has thrown this worldview into confusion. In each of the major wars of the last decade a section of the left has effectively sided with imperialism because it equated undemocratic and authoritarian regimes that were the victims of imperialism with imperialism itself. For Fred Halliday, a longtime opponent of imperialism, for instance, Saddam Hussein's Iraq was such an unacceptable regime that it justified the full onslaught of the greatest military powers in the world. For Mark Seddon, editor of *Tribune*, and many others on the left the nature of the Milosevic regime justified the imperialist bombing campaign against Serbia. And today many on the left found the Taliban such a uniquely reactionary regime that it justified the US and British war against Afghanistan.

The most elementary logical distinctions, if nothing else, seem to have been overridden in these arguments. For instance, one does not have to be a supporter of any of these regimes—indeed, one can be politically opposed to them all—and still maintain opposition to imperialist intervention. The basic principle of the rights of nations to self determination requires us to allow the exploited and oppressed people of these nations to settle accounts with their own tyrants. No one, either on the left or the right, suggested during the long and bloody history of the apartheid regime in South Africa that the appropriate response to such tyranny was to let loose the armed forces of America or Britain. Any imperial intervention, as long experience in Africa has taught us, would not help. Only the acts of the working people of South Africa, even if their struggle was long and pitted with setbacks, could ultimately bury the regime. The left internationally could and did aid this struggle, thus banishing the accusation that respecting the rights of nations to self determination is to abandon the local populations to the mercy of their dictators.

Neither, for most of the Stalinist-influenced left, were these criteria ever applied evenly. There is, for instance, a dictatorial regime ruled by an authoritarian figurehead with a well developed cult of the personality, that suppresses freedom of speech, exploits the workers and peasants, and puts into concentration camps individuals of whose sexual orientation it disapproves. The regime is Fidel Castro's Cuba. None of this should detract from the left's desire to oppose US imperialism's attempt to overthrow the Cuban regime, but it should guide us in how we handle similarly authoritarian regimes that do not happen to adopt progressive rhetoric.

Such regimes are likely to multiply in number. The state capitalist model of development is much less common. Anti-colonial struggles have given rise to ruling classes of new nations who now increasingly try to carve their own space in the world system by striking deals with the major powers. Such arrangements are, of course, no guarantee that today's imperial ally will not turn into tomorrow's imperial victim—as Saddam Hussein, Slobodan Milosevic and Mullah Omar can all testify. But what this illustrates is that we cannot decide whether or not to oppose imperialism simply on whether or not we find the past or present behaviour of the regime to be progressive.

In the era before the rise of Stalinism this was more clearly understood, at least on the revolutionary left. Writing in the early 1920s Georg

Lukács commented on the fact the 19th century 'movements for unity of Germany and Italy were the last of these objectively revolutionary struggles' for national liberation. The difference with modern struggles for national liberation, Lukács observed, is that they are now:

> *...no longer merely struggles against their own feudalism and feudal absolutism—that is to say only implicitly progressive—for they are forced into the context of imperialist rivalry between world powers. Their historical significance, their evaluation, therefore depends on what concrete part they play in the concrete whole.*[37]

It follows that:

> *Forces that work towards revolution today may very well operate in the reverse direction tomorrow. And it is vital to note that these changes...are determined decisively by the constantly changing relations of the totality of the historical situation and the social forces at work. So that it is no very great paradox to assert that, for instance, Kemel Pasha may represent a revolutionary constellation of forces in certain circumstances whilst a great 'workers' party' may be counter-revolutionary.*[38]

Lukács is generalising from positions developed by Lenin during the First World War. Lenin, for instance, was well aware of the shortcomings of the national bourgeoisie in the oppressed countries:

> *Not infrequently...we find the bourgeoisie of the oppressed nations **talking** of national revolt, while in practice it enters into reactionary compacts with the bourgeoisie of the oppressor nation behind the backs of, and **against**, its own people. In such cases the criticism of revolutionary Marxists should be directed not against the national movement, but against its degradation, vulgarisation, against the tendency to reduce it to a petty squabble.*[39]

Consequently Lenin was determinedly opposed to those on the left who qualified their opposition to imperialism on the basis that those facing imperialism did not hold progressive ideas:

> *To imagine that social revolution is **conceivable**...without revolutionary outbursts by a section of the petty bourgeoisie **with all its prejudices**, without a movement of the politically non-conscious proletarian and semi-proletarian masses...is to **repudiate social revolution**...[which] **cannot be** anything other than an outburst of mass struggle on the part of all and sundry oppressed and discontented elements. Inevitably...they will bring into the movement their prejudices, their revolutionary fantasies, their weaknesses and errors. But*

> **objectively** *they will attack* **capital**...
>
>   *The dialectics of history are such that small nations, powerless as an* **independent** *factor in the struggle against imperialism, play a part as one of the ferments, one of the bacilli, which help the* **real** *anti-imperialist force, the socialist proletariat, to make its appearance on the scene.*[40]

We do not live in the era of the Russian Revolution, but it is still true that whether or not we oppose imperialism is determined by the totality of relations in the system at any one point, and not only by the internal character of the regimes that find themselves, however ineffectively, opposed to imperialism.

Imperialism, anti-imperialism and socialism

Imperialism is an evolving system. Since the very earliest days of capitalism, international expansion has been written into its structure. The union with Scotland and the colonisation of Ireland formed one of the first capitalist states, Britain. Both events were decisively shaped by the revolution of the 17th century. And one of Britain's first post-revolutionary wars was with the second major capitalist state of the day, the Dutch republic. Emerging capitalist states and declining pre-capitalist empires fought for dominance in America, Africa, Asia and the Far East. For two centuries British, Dutch, French, German, Italian and other major powers struggled to conquer the globe, and subdue indigenous populations and minor powers.

The apogee was reached in the 20th century as wholly capitalist powers clashed in two world wars, and again and again in countless colonial conflicts. At the beginning of the century Lenin and Bukharin outlined the two contradictory drives that still dominate the modern capitalist system. Bukharin wrote, 'Together with the internationalisation of economy and the internationalisation of capital, there is going on a process of "national" intertwining of capital, a process of "nationalising" capital, fraught with the greatest consequences'.[41] Globalisation on the one hand and the massive military-industrial network of the modern state on the other are the modern form of this contradiction. The result is that economic competition and the inequality and instability it creates constantly reproduce military competition and war. The drive to war has broken apart and reconstituted the imperialist system throughout the 20th century.

Since the Second World War formal colonies have largely gained their independence. Oppressed nations have come and gone, fought their battle, and joined the international system of states in more or less subordinate ranks. This process began with the American colonies in the 1770s and ran through to the liberation of Ireland and India, among many others, in the 20th century. But that does not mean that the national question has disappeared—merely that it has, like imperialism itself, evolved new forms. The indigenous ruling classes that took the place of their colonial overlords have often struggled to suppress new nationalist forces within their, often artificial, boundaries. So it was, for instance, that the new post-independence Indonesian ruling class fought to suppress the East Timorese. Equally these new ruling classes have struggled with the still ever-present economic and military strength of the major powers. And this returns us to the need, as Lukács argued, to assess each anti-imperial struggle from the standpoint of the whole contemporary alignment of forces in the imperialist system.

There is, however, one relatively consistent social position from which this assessment can best be carried out. As their rulers and would-be rulers twist and turn between colonialism and independence, accommodation and belligerence, the inescapable power of the international economy and the weight of the great states bear down on the workers and peasants of these societies. It is here that we find the one great enduring force opposed to the imperial system throughout its long evolution. Whatever its changing shape—from the primitive accumulation of the slave trade, through the early colonies, to the great imperial wars of the 20th century—these classes have stood in opposition to the system. Their struggle has certainly not always been victorious. It has often lain dormant for great lengths of time. But it has, nevertheless, risen again and again to confront both the imperial powers and the capitalist system from which they grew.

Karl Marx made the essential point that no matter how much the spread of capitalist relations may transform the economic structure of what is now called the Third World, no matter how many nations attain independence, the fundamental task of human liberation still falls to working people. Writing of British rule in India he argued:

> *All the English bourgeoisie may be forced to do will neither emancipate nor materially mend the social condition of the mass of the people, depending not only on the development of the productive powers, but on their appropriation by the people. But what they will not fail to do is to lay down the material premises for both. Has the bourgeoisie ever done more? Has it ever effected a progress without dragging individuals and peoples through blood and dirt, through misery and degradation?*
>
> *The Indians will not reap the fruits of the new elements of society scattered among them by the British bourgeoisie till in Great Britain itself the now ruling classes have been supplanted by the industrial proletariat, or till the Hindus themselves shall have grown strong enough to throw off the English yoke.*[42]

The British were eventually driven from India, but the fundamental task that Marx outlined remains unfinished. Since Marx's day the working class in India and elsewhere in the Third World has grown to be able to take a much more prominent role in dealing with the inheritors of imperial rule, be they indigenous bourgeoisies or new foreign powers. The growth of the international working class has, nevertheless, been a slow process. Workers are only now, perhaps, a majority of the world's oppressed and exploited. Various forms of 'extra-economic' coercion over labour remained a feature of the system well into the 20th century. In the less industrialised economies the working class is more differentiated into agricultural and semi-proletarian layers than elsewhere. And peasants still form a very large proportion of the world's oppressed and exploited. But for all this, as one important study shows, 'as the colonial era gave way to post-colonialism after the Second World War, so the traditional division of labour began to change. A substantial, if uneven, industrial development began in many areas of the Third World which significantly altered the social and economic conditions of labour'.[43] This was a new international division of labour that:

> ...fundamentally restructured the relations of production in the Third World, with the emergence of a substantial manufacturing sector oriented on the world market. The 'world market factories' carried out super-exploitation of their mainly female workers, but created the conditions for the emergence of a 'classical' confrontation between labour and capital.[44]

We have seen this long term economic process of class formation begin to express itself, albeit unevenly, in class consciousness and class organisation. If we think of the unions in countries as distant as South Africa, South Korea, Brazil and Indonesia we can see the possibilities. And, as part of this process of class organisation, political consciousness and political, sometimes overtly socialist, organisations have begun to grow. These currents are by no means homogeneous, even among socialists, where reformist and revolutionary alternatives both exist. And socialism, however defined, is by no means the only or the major set of ideas contending to express resistance to the system. Nationalism and Islamic ideas, to mention only two of the most prominent trends, command the support of many millions of workers, peasants and the poor around the globe.

Nevertheless, socialists do have a better chance than for many generations to build support for their views. Globalisation has created an international working class bigger than at any time in the history of capitalism. But it has failed to create a system that can sustain an acceptable livelihood for millions of workers. One consequence of this is a renewed drive to war characteristic of the contemporary imperial structure. The fall of Stalinism means that there is no ideological enemy to blame. This situation has therefore created a crisis of confidence in the system. The physical expression of this crisis is the international anti-capitalist movement.

It is in this anti-capitalist movement, now arguing its way to also being an anti-imperialist movement, that socialists can begin to win a much wider audience for the idea that working people have the power to overthrow the rule of capitalism and imperialism. Moreover, they can begin to successfully advance the view that the system can be replaced with an international system of co-operative labour so organised that it meets the needs of those who produce social wealth. The alternative is that we to allow our rulers to continue the routine business of imperialism—the organisation of human misery.

Notes

1 R Leger Sivard, *World Social and Military Expenditures 1996* (Washington, 1996), p17.

2 M Parvizi Amineh, *Towards the Control of Oil Resources in the Caspian Region* (New York, 1999), pp5-6.

3 Ibid, pp7-8.

4 Ibid, pp6-7.

5 Ibid, p11.

6 B Sutcliffe, *100 Ways of Seeing an Unequal* (London, 2001), p14.

7 Quoted in A G Frank, 'Caspian Sea Oil, Still the Great Game for Central Eurasia', a review essay of M P Croissant and B Aras (eds), *Oil and Geopolitics in the Caspian Sea Region* (Westport, Conn, and London, 1999), http://csf.colorado.edu/archive/agfrank

8 W J Clinton, 'On Track In Kosovo Toward Balkan Renaissance', *International Herald Tribune*, 24 May 1999.

9 'We have demonstrated that we were willing to undertake military action, not to seize territory, not for expansion, not for mineral resources. There is no oil in Kosovo...there is only some dirty lignite.' Robin Cook, interviewed by John Lloyd, *New Statesman*, 5 July 1999, p19.

10 A Rashid, *Taliban: Oil, Islam and the New Great Game in Central Asia* (London, 2000), p144.

11 M Parvizi Amineh, op cit, pp82-84.

12 H Pinter, 'The NATO Action in Serbia', in T Ali (ed), *Masters of the Universe? NATO's Balkan Crusade* (London, 2000), p333.

13 Quoted in 'Caspian Pipeline Tug Of War: Washington Favours Geopolitics Over Economics', *International Herald Tribune*, 9 November 1998.

14 Quoted in A Rashid, op cit, p156.

15 Strategic Forecasts report, 'Ajerbaijan Forces Pipeline Issue' (1999), www.stratfor.com

16 US Trade and Development Agency press release, 2 June 1999.

17 See A G Frank, op cit.

18 'Racing For Arms', *The Economist*, 5 June 1999. For more detail see J Rees, 'Oil, Gas and NATO's New Frontier', *New Political Economy*, vol 5, no 1 (March 2000), pp100-104.

19 Quoted in A G Frank, op cit.

20 Quoted ibid.

21   See International Institute for Strategic Studies, *Strategic Survey 2000/2001* (London, 2001), p63.
22   Ibid.
23   K Weisbrode, *Central Eurasia: Prize or Quicksand?*, International Institute for Strategic Studies, Adelphi Paper 338 (London, 2001), p23.
24   Ibid, p24.
25   See G Achcar, 'Rasputin Plays at Chess: How the West Blundered Into a New Cold War', in T Ali (ed), op cit, pp66-72.
26   Ibid, p72.
27   Quoted in A Rashid, op cit, p130.
28   D Johnstone, 'Humanitarian War: Making the Crime Fit the Punishment', in T Ali (ed), op cit, p154.
29   G Achcar, op cit, p74.
30   For a more elaborated account of this process, see J Rees, 'The New Imperialism', in *Marxism and the New Imperialism* (London, 1994), pp67-71.
31   See K Weisbrode, op cit, p19.
32   Ibid, pp19-20.
33   Ibid, p20.
34   J Rees, 'The New Imperialism', op cit, p117.
35   Ibid, p121.
36   J Wilson, S Goldenberg, E MacAskill, J Steele, 'New Brothers in Arms—Cans and Intelligence', *The Guardian*, 20 October 2001.
37   G Lukács, *Lenin: A Study in the Unity of his Thought* (London, 1977), p46.
38   G Lukács, *History and Class Consciousness* (London, 1971), p311.
39   V I Lenin, *Collected Works*, vol 23 (Moscow, 1964), p61.
40   Ibid, vol 22, pp355-357.
41   N Bukharin, quoted in A Brewer, *Marxist Theories of Imperialism: A Critical Survey* (London, 1980), p106.
42   K Marx, quoted ibid, p58.
43   R Munck, *The New International Labour Studies* (London, 1988), p33.
44   Ibid.

The long torment of Afghanistan

JONATHAN NEALE

Over the last 30 years the great and small powers of this world have made a hell of Afghanistan.[1]

In the summer of 1972 I was an anthropologist doing fieldwork in Afghanistan. I went to visit a friend from a poor nomad family in the TB sanatorium in Kabul. It was the only such facility in Afghanistan, and I had used what influence I had to get him admitted. We chatted with the other patients. He asked me for money to pay bribes to the hospital cooks so they would give him meals. I expressed surprise that he had to pay bribes even for that. 'Afghanistan, Zulumistan,' another patient said. It was a proverb: 'The land of the Afghans, the land of tyrants.' We all laughed. It was an angry laugh.

His aunt Miriam had lost her husband a few years before. A man had been robbed and killed near their small camp of nomad tents on the outskirts of Kabul. The police took Miriam's husband away on suspicion, because he was a poor man and a stranger. The next day they delivered him back to the camp, his body black from beating, his stomach split open, dead. The police told Miriam he had died from eating bad watermelon. What outraged her more than their little joke was that when the police brought the body to her, they dropped it on the ground rather than putting it down gently. There was nothing she could do.

That was in the time of King Zahir Shah. He ruled with the support of money and arms from both the US and the Soviet Union, trying to play them off against each other and stay neutral. At times under Zahir Shah there was brutal repression, with death squads coming for political opponents in the night. At times there was a form of limited democracy, without free elections and with political prisoners, but not with widespread killings. Miriam's husband was killed during a democratic period.

Power in Afghanistan then lay in the countryside, with big feudal landowners.[2] In each village one or a few families owned much of the land. Then there was a minority of families who farmed their own land, and perhaps employed one sharecropper. The majority in the countryside worked as sharecroppers. In the poorer lands around Kandahar the sharecropper got a third of the crop and the landowner two thirds. On the richer irrigated land around Jalalabad, the sharecropper got a fifth of the crop, or food for one person while working plus one ninth of the crop.

Whatever the share, the income of a shepherd, a sharecropper or a manual worker in the city usually worked out at enough to buy five pounds of wheat flour a day—2,400 calories each for two adults and 1,600 calories each for two children—and nothing else.

Roughly 2 percent of the land could be farmed (all statistics on Afghanistan, then and now, are guesses). Much of the rest of the country was desert or barren mountains, although parts of that were suitable for grazing sheep. Since 1838 the power of the king had rested on two pillars. One was the support of the feudal lords, the men who owned a large part of one village or several villages. These men ruled by force, with armed retinues. Traditionally they paid little tax, and by 1972 they paid none. The king could not insist they pay, so the other pillar of the regime was always a subsidy from abroad.[3]

In the early 19th century Afghanistan had ruled the fertile plains of Peshawar and Kashmir, in what are now India and Pakistan.[4] After they lost these to the Sikh kingdom, the Afghan state could never again support itself. The British Indian army invaded Afghanistan in 1838. The feudal lords took bribes to hand power to Britain. The people, deserted by their leaders, rose under the banner of Islam and drove the British out. Britain then put the old ruler, Dost Mohammed, back in power with a British subsidy.

In 1878 the British invaded again. This time too the feudal lords sold themselves and the people rose. Britain put a new and particularly brutal ruler, Abdur Rahman, in power. He used British money and British rifles to conquer the northern half of what is now Afghanistan, the central mountains of the Hazarajat, and the independent regions of Nuristan and Pakhtia along the Pakistani border. The modern Afghan state and its borders are the result of these conquests.

In 1919 a new ruler, Amanullah, took advantage of the unrest in India to go to war with British India in the Third Afghan War, and won full independence. The British cut off his subsidy. Amanullah, unable to break the feudal lords, had to try to raise taxes from the peasantry. They rose, again under the banner of Islam.

Amanullah was driven from Kabul in 1929. Nine months later Nadir Shah, one of his relatives, retook Kabul with British money and British arms. Britain continued to subsidise Nadir, and his son Zahir Shah, until 1947. After that the Soviet Union and the US competed to subsidise the Afghan government.

The Afghans had fought three holy wars against the British invaders, and one holy war against Amanullah. The Pashtuns along the other side of the border had resisted the British in innumerable small wars. There had also been a non-violent mass movement, the Servants of God, allied with Gandhi's congress and based on poor peasants and workers, that dominated Pashtun resistance in India from 1919 to 1947.

When the British first invaded Afghanistan in 1838, the Pashtuns there had a reputation in South Asia for being very relaxed about their Islam. By 1939 Afghanistan had a tradition that when the kings and feudal lords failed the common people they would resist under the banner of Islam. In 1838 the drawings of Pashtuns show men with glorious long hair hanging down their backs. By 1972 Pashtun men wore their hair cropped almost to the head, and eastern and southern Afghanistan were strongly Islamic areas. There was nothing Pashtun or Afghan about this—it was the result of fighting the British.

Somewhere between 40 and 50 percent of Afghans are Pashtuns, who speak the Pashtu language. There are several large minorities. The Tajiks in the east, north and west speak Farsi (Persian). The Uzbeks in the north speak a Turkish language. The Hazaras, the poorest of all, live in the central mountains and migrate to work in the cities. They speak Farsi. There are also smaller minorities—Nuristani, Khirgiz, Turkmen, Baluch, Pashai, and many more.

In 2001 much of Afghan politics is conventionally explained in ethnic terms. But until 1988 there were the Islamists on the right, the feudal powers led by the king, and the Communists. Afghan politics was about class. It was only after the Afghan people had been comprehensively betrayed and abused, first by the lords, then by the Communists and then by the Islamists, that people turned to ethnicity to organise.

The government of Zahir Shah did not develop the country. Cities, industry and workers would have destroyed the regime, and they knew it.[5] In 1972 there were only 30,000 industrial workers and miners in the whole country. But the government did spend money on schools, and on the university in Kabul. These schools produced a new class. Because there were so few people in the feudal families, most of the newly educated were the children of small farmers and shopkeepers, people with their own land and a sharecropper or two. These boys and girls took with them to school their parents' hatred of the feudal lords and the regime. In the cities, and particularly at Kabul University, they also learned to despise the old ways of the countryside. After education they took jobs as teachers in the schools, officers in the army, health professionals and civil servants. There they were paid three or four times the income of a manual worker or sharecropper, but in most cases little or no more than their fathers earned in the village. Both the Communists and the Islamists come from this new class.

The Communists were brave men and women, the flower of their generation. In the autumn of 1971 I stood on a street in Lashkargah, in the south, and watched a demonstration of high school students. They took turns standing on a box and giving speeches. The speeches were all slogans, and the main slogan was 'Death to the khans'. The khans were the local landlords. This was not an abstract slogan. The boys meant death to certain specific men they all knew, whose supporters watched the demonstration. On the edges of the street, peasant men watched, silent, their faces blank, for if they supported those boys they could easily be taken away in the night.

The Communists wanted to take the land from the khans. They wanted freedom and equality for women. They wanted a modern developed economy and an end to corruption. In the countryside, even in Lashkargah, the Communists could build support in the secondary schools. But in the villages the mullahs said the Communists were godless, which was true. The khans terrified those sharecroppers who might join the Communists. Under Zahir Shah a man could easily die for speaking out of turn in the village. The Communists won some respect, but they could not organise in the villages strongly enough to win the argument against the mullahs and khans.

In Kabul it was different. In the early 1950s, and again in the 1960s, there were relatively free elections. In the rural areas, and most cities, no one opposed to the local rich could stand, but in Kabul the Communists could. That is important—50 years ago, in 1951, the Communists won seats in Kabul. Afghanistan is a sink of reaction now not because it always has been, but because of what has happened since.

At Kabul University in 1971 the Communists came up against the Islamists. These were not traditional Muslims.[6] Traditional Afghan Islam leant heavily towards Sufi mysticism and worship at the graves of saints. The Islamists despised this village Islam. They took their politics from the Muslim Brotherhood in Egypt, and the ideas coming from the Al Azhar mosque and university in Cairo. They looked forward to a deeply changed Afghanistan, even as they said it would be like the time of the prophet. They, like the Communists, were a modern movement of the newly educated. Of their two most important young leaders, Gulbuddin

Hekmatyar and Ahmed Shah Massoud, both studied engineering at Kabul University. They were not mullahs.

The Communists and Islamists both hated the royal government and the stink of corruption, but they differed on three things. The Communists wanted to share out the land, while the Islamists defended property. The Communists wanted equality for women, and the Islamists were against it (women joined both groups, but they played a far larger and braver part in the Communist movement). And the Communists looked to Russia, while the Islamists looked to support from Saudi Arabia, and later the US. In 1972 the Communists and Islamists fought with guns on the campus of Kabul University, and the Islamists won. The Communists took the fighting to the secondary schools. There the students were poorer and fought with hatchets. The Communists had more support in the secondary schools because they were poorer.

In 1972 there was drought in the centre and north of the country. The nomads lost their sheep, and then the harvest failed. The US sent grain in aid. In towns in the north the district officers put the grain in piles in the centre of the town, guarded by soldiers. The local merchants then sold that grain at ten times the usual rate. Small farmers sold their fields at much below the usual rate to pay for that grain. Sharecroppers, shepherds and their families starved. A French journalist passing through asked starving people why they did not simply storm the piles of grain. 'The king has planes,' they explained. 'If we do, the government will bomb us'.[7] Those planes were Russian MIGs. The pilots were trained in Texas. Afghanistan was neutral. No one knows how many died in that famine, but it meant that when a coup ousted King Zahir the next year no one came to his defence.

Daoud, the uncle of King Zahir Shah, led the 1973 coup. Daoud's government leaned toward the Soviet Union in foreign policy. The Communists were now split into two factions. The more moderate *Parcham* (Flag) supported Daoud. *Parcham* were particularly strong in Kabul, and among the upper reaches of the middle class. The more radical faction, *Khalk* (People), opposed Daoud and went underground. They were stronger among the educated children of small peasants, and in the small towns. The *Khalk* were more Pashtun, the *Parcham* more Farsi speaking. This was because of their different class bases, not because of ethnicity.

Daoud used the *Parcham* Communists to break the Islamists, whose leaders were driven into exile in Pakistan in 1975. Then one night in April 1978 Daoud sent his police to arrest and either kill or imprison all the leading Communists in Kabul.[8] Daoud's coup in 1973 had been based on the army. The Communists had also been building support, and secret organisation, in the armed forces. The younger army officers were from the same educated new class as the Communists. The night that Daoud turned on the Communists they replied with a coup.

Only around Jalalabad was there any fighting. For the rest, nobody supported Daoud, as nobody had supported his nephew Zahir Shah. But the Communists had not won the political argument in the villages. Afghanistan had a conscript army. There were men from every village in Afghanistan in that army, most of them poor men who felt like the men in that TB hospital—'The land of the Afghans, the land of tyrants.' But instead of organising those conscripts against their officers, the Communists had organised a coup by the officers.

It's not hard to understand why they chose a revolution from the top. That was the prevailing radical politics of the time. Communists and radicals all over the world looked to the dictatorships of Russia, China, Vietnam and Cuba, all of them run from the top down. All over the Middle East radicals had tried to come to power through coups. In 1972 the idea of a revolution for democratic workers' power was a small enough tendency that few, if any, people in Afghanistan had heard of it. This was not only true in Kabul. Of the three leaders of the revolution, Karmal learned his politics in Afghanistan, Taraki in Bombay and Amin in New York. In each case the ideas available to them were those of Stalin, Mao and Castro.

When the Communists took power in 1978 their first two acts were to decree land reform and abolish the payment of bride price at a marriage. Both were symbolic statements. They had to be enforced in the villages. When the Communists came to the village with their new policies they came in the jeeps of the old government, in the uniforms of officers and the Western clothes of the old ruling class. Soon they faced rebellion, beginning in Pakhtia and Nuristan along the Pakistani border. These were areas where people could remember freedom from any central government. From there the revolt spread across the rural areas. It is difficult to tell who led this revolt, but the banner was Islam. The historical tradition was that a people whose feudal leaders had deserted them fought on as Muslims. The mullahs now said that the Communists were puppets of the Russians.

The Communists turned to arrests and torture because they had not won the argument in the villages. That made more enemies. And when the Communists lost control of an area they fell back on the methods of the old government—guns and bombs. It is not possible to wage class war by bombing a village. The bombs hit everyone, and unite them. In one area after another the Communists found themselves fighting the people they had meant to free.

By late 1979, a year and a half after coming to power, the Communist regime was clearly about to fall. Desperate, the *Parcham* and *Khalk* factions began to kill and imprison each other. At this point the Soviet Union invaded to keep the Communists in power. It did not do so for the sake of the Afghans. The Soviet Union had four Central Asian republics bordering Afghanistan—what are now the countries of Uzbekistan, Turkmenistan, Tajikistan and Kirghizstan. The majority in these countries was at least nominally Muslim,[9] and there was a growing Islamist feeling against Russian rule. If Afghanistan fell to Muslim insurrection, they might follow. And Soviet Central Asia contained much of Russia's oil and gas.

When the Russian tanks rolled in and the planes landed, the Communists accepted their support. They did not welcome it. The Russians had to kill President Amin, the leader of the *Khalk*, and replace him with Karmal, the *Parchami* leader. Many Communists deserted to the resistance or went into exile. Many *Khalkis* continued in government but told those close to them how much they resented the Russians. Many *Khalkis* were imprisoned by Karmal. But as an organised force, both the *Khalki* and *Parchami* Communists served under the Russians and fought alongside them.

Quite rapidly, though, most of the people who had supported the Communists turned against them. The Islamists, the village mullahs and the old landlords had said the Communists were just tools of the Russians. Now people could see they were right. The base of the Communists had been in the cities. In the spring of 1980 people went up onto the roofs of their houses at night in Herat, Afghanistan's third city. From the roofs they all shouted 'God is great' into the darkness. It was calculated defiance—the army and the Russians could not attack a whole city for shouting that. The protest spread to Kandahar, the second city, and then to Kabul, the capital.[10] There, the civil servants, who had been the Communists' strongest supporters, went on strike in protest at the Russians. For years the students at the girls' high school had led the campaign against the veil, marching through the streets, braving the mullahs who threw acid at their legs. Now the girls at the high school demonstrated in the schoolyard, calling on the men of Afghanistan to fight the invader, as women had done against the British invaders.

There were eight years of bitter war. Because the resistance had the support of the people, the Russians could only fight back with firepower. They used bombers, strafing planes, hundreds of thousands of land mines, helicopter gunships and napalm. No one knows how many people died in the war. Nobody was counting. Some Islamists say 2 million people out of a population of 15 or 20 million. They probably exaggerate. The more usually accepted figure is 1 million, though that too is only a guess. Perhaps it was only half a million.

About 6 million villagers became refugees. Two million went to

Pakistan, where they lived on handouts in mud and tent camps. Two million went to Iran, where there were no camps and no relief, but where many found jobs as casual building labourers and the like. A million or so took refuge in Kabul, whose population swelled from half a million to 2 million. Many internal refugees went to other cities, and many people lost arms, legs or eyes to landmines.

This Russian war destroyed Communism and socialism in the hearts of Afghans. If we take the figure of 1 million dead, that is 200 times the number killed on 11 September 2001 in New York. Afghanistan's population is less than a tenth of the US's. That means the impact of the Russian war was 2,000 times the impact of New York on Americans. If we take the lowest possible figure, half a million dead, that is still 100 times the number dead in New York, in less than a tenth of the population, for 1,000 times the impact. This is not to diminish in any way the carnage or the grief in New York. It is only to make concrete what that same carnage and grief, on a far greater scale, must have felt like in Afghanistan. It also suggests what the return of the bombers must feel like to Afghans now.

The resistance to the Russian invasion was quite unlike that in the guerrilla wars in Vietnam, Algeria, Yemen, Zimbabwe or Malaysia. In all those places the guerrillas were united under one political and military leadership. In Afghanistan the building blocks of the resistance were the local *qaums*.[11]

The best translation of *qaum* into English is community. It can mean a small tribe, an ethnic group, a linguistic group, a religious sect, three hamlets or the followers of one landlord. Sometimes a small valley can be a *qaum*. More usually, there are several *qaums* in a valley. In Dar-e-Nur, in Ningrahar, for instance, in 1972 there were several *qaums*. Three small settlements of Pashtu-speaking nomads formed three different *qaums*. There were other Pashtun farmers of the Safi tribe, living in the lower part of the valley, and several communities of Pashai speakers living in the centre and higher reaches of the valley. In the largest village the people were split between hamlets loyal to one political leader and those loyal to another.[12]

During the resistance to the Russians, some of these *qaums* combined together to fight, and some did not. When the Russians came, the men of the *qaum*, or several *qaums*, would fight. But when the Russians left, nobody pursued them. A *qaum* who lived near a road would venture out to ambush a Russian column and then run away. But beyond that there was no co-ordinated military action.[13]

The resistance of the *qaums* inside Afghanistan called themselves the Mujahadeen, the people of the jihad. They were consciously continuing the tradition of holy war against the British invaders. The formal leadership of the Mujahadeen fell to seven different Islamist political parties, all based in Peshawar in Pakistan. The governments of Pakistan, Saudi Arabia and the US supported the Peshawar parties. Inter Services Intelligence, the secret police of the Pakistani army, did most of the organising on the ground. Pakistan was a military dictatorship under General Zia in these years, and the ISI grew to become one of the great powers in the land. Saudi Arabia provided much of the money for the resistance. The US provided some of the money, and many of the weapons were arms from the Arab countries and Israel, paid for by the US. The CIA organised US support for the Mujahadeen in Pakistan.

US policy in the early 1980s was to use the resistance to harry and destabilise Russia as part of the Cold War. It was not that they particularly favoured the Islamists in the resistance. Rather, they were using the stick to hand to beat Russia. Much of the Pakistani military, and the Saudi government, were more committed to Islamic reaction.

The money and guns were paid out to the leaders of the seven Islamist parties in Peshawar. Some of the weapons and money were then sent on to the local Mujahadeen resistance groups inside Afghanistan. In return, the leader of the local groups would declare his allegiance to that Peshawar party, while the leaders of rival local groups would ally themselves with other parties. Local leaders often changed parties, taking their following with them. The Peshawar party did not give orders to the local group, did not control the whole of any one area, and did not co-ordinate the resistance. The leaders of the Peshawar Islamist parties all kept a considerable proportion of the foreign money for themselves. Within four years both the Afghan refugees in Pakistan and the fighters inside the country were deeply cynical about the Peshawar Islamists.

These local leaders were usually not the old feudal lords of the valleys. Most of those people had fled to Pakistan, and often eventually to the US to begin new lives. It is difficult to tell who now controlled the land. I have not been back to Afghanistan since 1973. No reporter, no academic and no Afghan source I can find seems to have asked who controlled the land. In a peasant society this is an astonishing omission. So we have to guess.

My guess for the period of resistance to the Russians is that much of the land formerly controlled by the old feudal lords, and by other refugees, fell under the control of the new local leaders of the Mujahadeen resistance. They were opposed to land reform, and so there was probably little sharing out. At the same time, the only way to back up their new land ownership was force. The old feudal lords had effectively ruled through retinues of local gunmen. The new lords would have done the same, and handed some of the land to these gunmen.

With the new resistance came a new crop—opium. Afghanistan had for many years exported opium on a small scale. In 1972 I had seen it growing in small amounts on the American irrigation project in Helmand and the Russian irrigation project near Jalalabad, and in large amounts along the Pakistani border. Now opium growing exploded, and heroin processing plants were built in both Pakistan and Afghanistan.

This was possible because in most rural areas there was now no central government to stop poppy growing. On irrigated land the same constant sunlight that makes Afghanistan ideal for growing grapes and melons also makes it ideal for poppies. But the real change was in Pakistan. There the Pakistani military and the CIA now allowed, and increasingly encouraged, the opium trade. They did so for several reasons. The peasant fighters of the resistance had to make a living in conditions where farming was difficult, and much of the land was mined. The CIA had done much the same in Indochina during the Vietnam War. It had encouraged opium cultivation by its client troops in Laos, and helped with the export of heroin through Vietnam. In South Vietnam President Thieu and Vice-President Ky had been central figures in the heroin trade. So the CIA was used to doing this.[14]

Also, the CIA was smuggling guns and arms on a large scale, though without an official budget to do so. The money had to come from somewhere. And wherever there are conduits for black money to aid rebels, the same lines of finance and money-washing are easily available to move drugs in the opposite direction.

The Pakistani military, and particularly the ISI, also had an increasing stake in the heroin trade. Many generals became fabulously rich. This deep corruption in the military has degraded social life in Pakistan. To be ruled by people who take bribes and steal from the public purse is one thing. To be ruled by an army full of narcotics criminals is quite another.

In the 1980s the CIA and the Saudis were also looking for ways to bring some order among the political parties, and some degree of control over them. One strand in this strategy was for the CIA to build up an organisation of Islamist volunteers, called al-Qaida, many of them from Saudi Arabia and the Gulf. The CIA's man in charge of this was Osama Bin Laden. He was paid, and funded, by the US. The son of a prominent Saudi construction magnate, Bin Laden came to Afghanistan originally at the urging of Saudi intelligence. But he was not simply an American puppet, any more than the Islamists in Peshawar were. For the moment his goals were the same as the US's, and he worked for them. Like the leaders of the Islamist parties, he ran his operation from Peshawar.[15]

Opinion was divided in the US government on how to support the resistance. The CIA, with a good idea of what was happening on the ground, was against giving too many weapons to the Mujahadeen resistance. It wanted to hurt Russia, but was worried about the consequences if the Islamist parties actually won. The Iranian Revolution and the rise to power of an Islamist government there had shaken the US government. In Palestine, Lebanon, Egypt, Saudi and North Africa, Islamist oppositions now appeared to be the main threat to the dictatorships of the Middle East and the US power that stood behind them. So the CIA did not want responsibility for a victorious and very right wing Islamist regime in Kabul.

Other power centres in Washington, and particularly the State Department, did want to arm the Afghan resistance heavily. Their thinking was that the damage to Russian power would outweigh any threat to US interests. In 1986 this wing of the US government won the argument, and the CIA began supplying large numbers of surface to air Stinger missiles to the resistance inside Afghanistan. These handheld Stingers could shoot down planes and helicopters. From 1986 on, Russia began to lose hundreds of aircraft and helicopters each year. The loss of life was important to the Russian government. More important was the stunning cost of replacing the aircraft. A large modern helicopter, let alone a bomber, costs millions. The war was now costing the Russian economy many billions.

In 1988 the Russian government under Gorbachev decided to leave Afghanistan. This was partly because Gorbachev was trying to rescue an imploding Soviet economy, and partly because it could not win against the considerable heroism of the Afghan people.

The government in Kabul was still led by the Communists. The Russians had replaced President Babrak with Najibullah, the former head of the secret police. Najibullah's enemies said that he personally presided over the death of 80,000 political prisoners in Kabul—Islamists, Communists, and many just caught up in the repression. I think this is probably a grossly inflated figure. But it is beyond doubt that Najibullah was a hands-on torturer and in charge of the deaths of tens of thousands. It was an index of the corruption of Afghan Communism that such a man could become leader. What made it even more macabre was that he was a doctor by profession.

In 1988 I expected that Najibullah's government would quickly fall to the Islamist resistance, and then the Islamists would fall out among themselves. In fact they fell out before they could take Kabul.[16] When the Russians left, the Peshawar Islamist parties combined for an assault on Kabul. Their first target was Jalalabad, the small Afghan city on the road from Peshawar to Kabul. They met unexpectedly fierce resistance from the Communist-led garrison there. Just as important, the local Mujahadeen resistance troops were now reluctant to fight.

For at least the previous two centuries, internal warfare in Afghanistan had been relatively limited. Where the forces of the central government confronted much smaller local forces, they had simply smashed them. But in civil wars Afghan armies mostly avoided large-scale battle. The war against Russia had been different. Here issues of principle, of religion, and of what class would own the land were dominant. The Afghan peasants had been willing to die in large numbers for what they believed in. But even then they had still not been prepared to attack outside their local areas.

The local Mujahadeen also had no respect for the Peshawar parties and the Islamists. They regarded the leaders of the parties as corrupt cowards who stole foreign aid while other people died for them. Now, in front of Jalalabad and then Kabul, the people who had been prepared to die against the Russians were not prepared to die for the Islamists. They had fought for the freedom of their valley, not for rule by new gangsters in Kabul.

The local leaders of the Mujahadeen probably had little interest in a strong central government. If I am right about them seizing much of the land, the establishment of central government in Kabul might well have meant the return of the old feudal landlords who would reclaim their land.

The Peshawar parties were falling out among themselves. Kabul, and all Afghanistan, was now the prize to reward whichever gangster could out-manoeuvre the others. The various parties began to shoot each other.

The people of Kabul, and to a lesser extent Jalalabad and Mazar in the north, had once supported the Communists. They had turned against them after the Russian invasion. With the invaders gone, however, the Communists now looked like a better bet than the corrupt Peshawar parties, themselves obviously the clients of Pakistan, Saudi Arabia and the US. So the Jalalabad garrison held on tenaciously, and the Mujahadeen assault failed. Kabul and much of the north remained in the hands of Najibullah. He began to present himself as a Muslim ruler, and made alliances with many of the old tribal lords and some of the new Mujahadeen landlords. Critically, he still had some Russian money and support. With the Soviet army gone, the CIA had won what it wanted, and cut off almost all its support to the Islamist parties. In 1988 Washington had no particular interest in an Islamist government in Kabul, but the Islamist parties still enjoyed Pakistani and Saudi backing though on nothing like the same scale. However, Najibullah's support slowly bled away.

Najibullah's single most important force was the Uzbek militia led by the Communist General Dostum. The majority Uzbek areas in the north of the country had come under Pashtun control in the 1880s. Uzbek peasants and lords had lost a considerable part of their land to Pashtun settlers who were planted there by the rulers in Kabul. This had been a running sore in the politics of northern Afghanistan, and under Dostum the Uzbeks got some of that land back. But Dostum could tell which way the wind was blowing. In 1992 he deserted Najibullah, and entered into an alliance with Ahmed Shah Massoud, the Islamist who controlled the Tajik, Persian-speaking valley of Panjshir just to the north of Kabul. Without the support of Dostum, Najibullah fell and Massoud's Panjshiri troops swept into Kabul.

Afghan politics was now divided along ethnic lines. There was nothing primordial or Afghan about this. Under the old regime the king, the commander of the army and the minister of the interior had always been Pashtuns. But the government had rested on an alliance of all the big landlords—Pashtun, Tajik, Uzbek and even Hazara. Significantly, the language of government, the university and the army had always been Persian, not Pashtu. Under the Communists, the presidents, army commanders and ministers of the interior had also been Pashtuns.[17] Again, however, the Communist base depended on a real alliance of Pashtuns, Uzbeks and Tajiks. The Islamists, too, had been an alliance of all the main ethnic groups. From 1950 to 1988 ethnicity had never ceased to matter. But national politics had been organised along lines of class and religion.

Now the Communists were utterly discredited. The Islamists were losing support. There was certainly no principled religious reason to support one Islamist group over another. More and more, the only basis left for political organising was ethnicity. The worst example of this was the degradation of the *Khalkis*. They had been the more radical of the Communist factions, more fiercely devoted to land reform and equality for women. As Najibullah fell, many of the *Khalki* army officers reinvented themselves as Pashtun chauvinists. Tajik and Uzbek Islamists now controlled Kabul. Many of the *Khalkis* went over to the side of Gulbuddin Hekmatyar, the leader of the most extreme Islamist party, and a Pashtun. The hard right and the hard left had joined forces as Pashtun chauvinists.

For the moment, the US government cared little about what happened. The Pakistani government still did. It was now an elected government led by Benazir Bhutto. A faction in the Pakistani army had blown up a plane containing the dictator, Zia, and several generals loyal to him, and handed power back to civilians. The army and the ISI, however, were still the power behind the parliamentary government. In Afghanistan they now supported Hekmatyar and his party.

Hekmatyar's forces occupied the hills above Kabul, trying to take power from the alliance of the Tajik Islamist Massoud and the Uzbek former Communist Dostum. The Russians had almost destroyed Kandahar, the second city, in the war. But Kabul still stood, unbombed. Now Hekmatyar unleashed Saudi and Pakistani supplied artillery on the houses of Kabul. Over four years he destroyed much of the city and killed an estimated 50,000 civilians.

Within Kabul, Massoud's Tajik forces now fought it out with the Islamists who controlled the Hazara neighbourhoods. The Hazaras had always been the most despised of Afghan minorities. They were Shias, unlike most Afghans. More important, their central mountain homeland, the Hazarajat, had the poorest land in Afghanistan. Many of them had to migrate to Kabul for work, where they were porters in the bazaar, servants and construction workers. But they had fought bravely, probably more bravely than anybody else, against the Russians. Now Massoud moved against them. He was beginning to get Russian money, and Iran supported the Hazara Islamists.

The ordinary people of Afghanistan had expected peace when the Russians left. Now they had unending war between unprincipled gangsters. Cynicism and a bitter hatred towards all their leaders became common currency. The local leaders of the resistance also earned people's hatred. They, and their armed retainers, abused people and stole. It was also alleged that in some areas they took the daughters of weaker people whenever they felt like it. I am not sure if this is true. In any case, if I am right that they had seized other people's land, their new holdings rested upon armed force, not legitimacy. They could only hold that land by obvious shows of their power.

In 1995, three years after Massoud swept into Kabul, a new force arose in the Pashtun south, around Kandahar, the second city—the Taliban. The Taliban said that all the Islamists and the local Mujahadeen leaders were corrupt. Most people agreed with that. The Taliban took their name from the talib students at the many small religious schools that trained mullahs. These schools had multiplied in Afghanistan, and even more around the Afghan refugee camps in Pakistan, with support from the Saudis. The Islam they taught was not the Islamism of the Peshawar parties, which had looked to Egypt and the Muslim Brotherhood. The Taliban ideology mixed three traditions the old village Islam of Afghanistan, the 10th century Wahabi reformism of Saudi Arabia, and the 19th century Indian Deobandi anti-colonial Islam. Massoud, Hekmatyar and the like had been university students. The talib students and the mullahs had a few years of schooling at most, and most of that in religious texts in Arabic. They seemed to represent a return to the Islamic practices under Zahir Shah in the 1950s and 1960s. However, the actual talib students were mostly boys from poor families, and many of them had only known the privation of the refugee camps.

These religious students formed the core of the Taliban troops. Most of them were too young to have fought in the war against the Russians. The leader of the Taliban was Mullah Omar, who had been a commander in the local Mujahadeen near Kandahar during the war against the Russians. He was a village mullah, from a poor family, with little education, blind in one eye from a war wound. His followers said he had founded the Taliban when two Mujahadeen commanders near Kandahar fought a tank battle over who would have sex with one particular boy. Mullah Omar had led the local rising against them.

The royal regime had been based on the landlords. The Communists and the Islamists were both led by the state petty bourgeoisie. Mullah Omar, it seemed, finally, was one of the people, leading an army of poor boys. He was heir to the old tradition of village religious resistance to the British.

The Taliban started at the Pakistani border, just south of Kandahar, and then swept north to take that city. Their base secure, they then attacked the Helmand valley to the west. This was the centre of opium poppy growing, controlled by the Akhundzada family. Fighting was heavy—poppies mattered. Then the Taliban took Herat, and the west. That base secure, the Taliban went north to the outskirts of Kabul. As they advanced, local resistance commanders came over to them without a shot fired. The Taliban had considerable legitimacy. It looked like the Taliban might be a force for honesty. They were also well armed and officered, and everybody knew they had the support of the Americans. The Taliban might bring what almost everybody now desperately wanted—peace.

Clinton's American government was supporting the Taliban because it too now wanted peace in Afghanistan—and a pipeline. With the collapse of the Soviet Union, the Soviet provinces of Central Asia, just to the north of Afghanistan, had become independent countries. Some of the old Soviet oilfields were now in four of those new countries— Azerbaijan, Uzbekistan, Turkmenistan and Kazakstan. Two of these bordered Afghanistan, all had at least nominally Muslim majorities, and all were ruled by former Communist politicians who had reinvented themselves as ethnic dictators. In the early 1990s the American oil companies began to move in, and it became clear that the Central Asian oil and gas reserves were far larger than had been thought. The figures are not reliable. Some sources say half of the world's oil reserves are in Central Asia, and some say a quarter or a fifth. The important thing was that it was not clear which oil powers would end up controlling the Central Asian reserves. The leading contenders were Russia, China, the US, Iran and, just possibly, Turkey.

The crucial issue was pipelines. Before the collapse of the Soviet Union all the pipelines had been built to carry the oil north to Russia. They are still there. In Soviet times the central government had paid far less than the world price for this oil. Now the new Russian government was still paying, in most cases, less than half the world price. The Central Asian regimes were looking for new pipelines that could carry their newly discovered resources to market for a better rate.

The US oil companies had problems with almost all the proposed pipelines. One way out ran through China. Then China would control the oil, and China was already becoming a competitor with US capital. Another proposed pipeline would run under the Caspian Sea north of Iran and then down through Chechnya, Georgia and Turkish Kurdistan to the Mediterranean. This was preferable to the US, but Russia would still control it if it ran Chechnya. An alternative could run across the Black Sea and down through Macedonia, quite near to Kosovo. Not entirely by coincidence, there were wars in Azerbaijan, Georgia, Chechnya, Turkish Kurdistan, Macedonia and Kosovo in the 1990s.

The Turkish and Black Sea pipelines, however, were going to be very expensive to build, and would run though many competing jurisdictions. The obvious alternative was a pipeline from Turkmenistan down through Iran to the Persian Gulf. This would be much shorter than the others, easy and much cheaper to build. Iran was politically stable, and already had tanker ports, refineries and a developed oil industry.

But Iran had been the US's enemy since 1980. The idea of Iran controlling Central Asian oil, or controlling it in alliance with the Central Asian countries, gave the US government fits. So it favoured another short, easy to build route through Afghanistan. That would run from Turkmenistan down through Herat in western Afghanistan to the coast of Pakistan. It was effectively the same route as the proposed Iranian pipeline, just 100 miles or so to the west. Technically it would be easy. An Argentinian oil company already had a contract with the government of Turkmenistan to build it. A US oil and gas company, UNOCAL, bribed the Turkmen government to give it the pipeline contract instead. Now the US corporations had their own proposed pipeline, and in time the possibility of becoming the major oil and gas power in Central Asia.

The problem was that there was no peace in Afghanistan. Nobody in their right mind would build a pipeline through all those competing Islamist warlords. The US needed a stable government, allied to it and to Pakistan, in control of Afghanistan. The Pakistani army and the ISI suggested the Taliban could provide this, and the American government decided they were the best option. The Pakistani army had concluded that there was no way Hekmatyar, its man up to that time, was going to win power. The Taliban might. With luck, this would give Pakistan a hand in Central Asian oil. Even without that, it would open new trade routes from Central Asia through Herat to Pakistan. For this reason, the Pakistani trucking companies were early supporters of the Taliban.

When the Pakistani army withdrew its support from Hekmatyar, he joined forces with Massoud in Kabul. It was regarded by all as a deeply unprincipled alliance. The man who had shelled Kabul for four years was now to be its saviour. Cynicism towards the Islamists reached new heights.

The pipeline and trade made Herat more important to the Pakistani and US governments than Kabul. So the Taliban took Herat first. Then they launched a serious assault on Kabul. Their army was a unity of several forces. Many of the rank and file were young talib students. The guns and ammunition came from Pakistan. The Taliban also had a large fleet of Datsun pickup trucks they used for mobile fighting in the western plains on the road to Herat, a bit like tank warfare. These pickups came from Saudi Arabia, and were effective against Islamist ground troops. The Taliban also fought with the discipline not of inexperienced boys, but of an army with officers experienced in conventional warfare. Some of these officers were Pakistani army men. Others were *Khalkis*, Pashtun former Communists, busy changing their names from Major Watandar to Mullah Mohammed (all Taliban commanders are Mullahs so and so, but not all were mullahs before). Massoud later said there were 6,000 *Khalkis* with the Taliban army. This is a wild exaggeration, but that there were many *Khalkis* with the advancing forces nobody but the Taliban disputes.

The Taliban also had large amounts of money. It was assumed in Afghanistan that this came from the Saudis and the US. This money was used to bribe key local leaders as their army swept north. In 1996 they drove Massoud and the Tajik Islamists out of Kabul, and pushed north.

Everywhere the Taliban took power they disarmed the population. This was new. Even under the king, many rural households had been armed. Since then the country had become awash with guns. The Taliban were promising the people the roads would be safe, and clear for Pakistani truckers. There would be no more roadblocks every few miles, levying tolls. The Mujahadeen leaders would no longer be able to seize land or use the sons and daughters of the peasantry for their sexual pleasures. (There is considerable question whether the Mujahadeen were in fact doing this. The war against the Russians, and the civil war that followed, had seen almost no military rape, by Afghans or Russians. This is in stark contrast to most wars.)

It seems that in many parts of Afghanistan people held their breath and hoped. Certainly no one seemed prepared to fight for the Islamists or the local Mujahadeen leaders. Even a bad peace can look better than 20 years of war.

The last city the Taliban had to take was Mazar-e-Sharif in the north. Again they did it without firing a shot. Dostum's second in command was bribed into handing over control of the city. For a day the Taliban ruled all but a few pockets of Afghanistan. It looked as if the Pakistani army had got its way, and the US government would recognise the Taliban.

Like Kabul, Mazar is a multi-ethnic city—Uzbek, Pashtun, Tajik and Hazara. The young Taliban soldiers now moved to disarm the population, as they had in other parts of the country. According to one report, the Taliban went armed into a Hazara mosque. The Hazaras there, appalled, refused to give up their guns. However the fighting started, the Hazaras of Mazar rose. As they fought the Taliban, the Tajiks and Uzbeks of Mazar rose with them. When they saw what was happening, so did the Pashtuns of Mazar.

The Hazaras had good reasons not to give up their guns. Pashtun nomad khans and government officials had long oppressed the Hazaras in their mountain homeland. For decades they had been the bottom of the hierarchy in Kabul and Mazar—manual workers. In the war against the Russians they had finally organised to control the central mountains, the Hazarajat, and win some dignity in the cities. Now all this was threatened. In Kabul the year before the leader of the Hazaras there had deserted Massoud and made an alliance with the Taliban. Taliban soldiers had taken him away and pushed him out of a helicopter to his death. Whatever the public face of the Taliban as strict Muslims, their main ideology was Pashtun chauvinism. So the Hazaras of Mazar rose.

The Taliban had battled in the west against Islamist forces. They had never met with, and could not comprehend, an urban working class rising. The Taliban fled, but many did not escape. Hundreds of Taliban boys were killed on the streets. Others were left in truck containers in the desert until they died of asphyxiation and heat. The Taliban replied with pogroms in the Hazara neighbourhoods of Kabul. Afghanistan had finally reached the depths of ethnic cruelty so long familiar in Europe and India.

In 1996 the Taliban finally retook Mazar. This time they murdered civilians in large numbers. And this time they raped. But they had lost US support. It was clear to the US government that the Taliban could not deliver permanent peace in Afghanistan. The pipeline was dead. The US government now leaned toward the Turkish pipeline, but also began to try to re-establish relations with Iran.

The Taliban, however, still had the support of Pakistan and Saudi Arabia. An opposition alliance held small parts of the north and east. This opposition is usually called the Northern Alliance, a name they would not use for themselves, since they claim to be the legitimate rulers of all Afghanistan. This alliance held perhaps 5 or 10 percent of the country. The Tajik Islamist Massoud and the Uzbek former Communist Dostum led them. Massoud had money and guns from Iran, Russia and India. Dostum was backed by the government of former Soviet Uzbekistan. India was on board as a way to make trouble for Pakistan, and because many of the militant guerrillas who faced the Indian army in Kashmir were allied to the Taliban and supported by the Pakistani army. But it is a measure of how discredited the Islamists had become that, even with all this money behind them, the Northern Alliance could only attract 5,000 fighters to their side.

The Taliban held most of Afghanistan. But in many ways foreign NGOs and aid agencies were the real government. The Islamists, Dostum's militia and the Taliban had controlled armies and the police. But to a certain extent after 1988, and to a very large extent after 1992, Western NGOs, mostly from the European Union and the United Nations, had delivered the other functions of government. The cities in particular were still full of refugees from the war, who had little prospect of going home. The Islamists and the Taliban did not raise taxes to feed the people. So the NGOs and the United Nations fed the poor. They also ran and funded the schools and hospitals. All the things for which people might be grateful they owed to these outsiders. All the things they might hate a government for—guns and bombs—they owed to the Islamists and the Taliban.

This goes some way to explaining the deeply reactionary version of Islam propounded by the Taliban in power. Everyone knew they had begun as clients of the non-Muslim US government, the corrupt Muslim state of Saudi Arabia, and the Pakistani army. Large sections of the Pakistani officer class may be right wing Islamists in a political sense, but no one thinks they are good Muslims. The Taliban were doing nothing for people, and beholden to bad Muslims or enemies of Islam. The only thing they had going for them ideologically was the rhetoric of Islam. And because they were so compromised, they emphasised that Islam by being more reactionary and more brutal than the Islamists.

Part of their version of Islam was sending women back to the home. Before explaining this, we need to clear away some lies. It is said now, on all sides, that the Taliban force all girls to leave school. They force all women to wear the *burqa*, the full body veil that makes a woman look like a ghost, seeing the world through a small mesh in front of her eyes. And it is said that this is done because it is traditional Pashtun village custom, and the Taliban are ignorant, medieval men who have taken their customs to the city.

None of these things are true, though each builds on a partial truth.[18] In the past, Pashtun women were no more likely to wear the full veil than other Afghan women. I lived in Pashtun villages from 1971 to 1973, both in the south near Kandahar and the east near Jalalabad. In both regions the women of a few rich families in each village lived in seclusion, covering their heads and bodies in public places, but rarely wearing a *burqa*. Some of these were big landlords, and some smaller peasants with their own land. In all cases, these were families rich enough that the women did not have to work. Poor people, they said, let their wives wander the village without shame. We, who are modest, keep ours locked up. The ideology of the Taliban is an ideology of a new rural elite, rich peasants who aspire to seclude their women.

In the large majority of peasant households, and in all nomad households, women had to work in the fields or with the animals. They might turn away or pull their headscarves across their faces when strangers approached. But the male strangers would turn away as a courtesy too, so as not to intrude on the women.

In the cities more people were able to depend only on the labour of men, and the full veil was more common among working class women. But the streets were full of working class women whose faces you could see, and many middle and upper class women in Western styles and trouser suits like their counterparts in the West.

In 2001 the Taliban enforced the veil in the cities. They did not enforce it in the Pashtun villages. There women still had to work. More important, the Taliban did not control the villages. They ruled over them but were not strong enough to impose their values. Had they done so, the villagers would have risen. In many Pashtun villages girls continued to go to school.

I write this in the third week of the fifth Afghan war. The US and British governments are bombing Kandahar. We are told that this is 'the spiritual home of the Taliban', because bombing that sounds better than bombing a city of a quarter of a million people. I watch the refugees coming to the Pakistani border from Kandahar on my television. They are mostly women and children, and the women are rarely fully veiled.

The oppression of women was real in the 1950s and 1960s. But there was space for resistance. At weddings, the men and women separately sang songs of illicit love. And older women could walk through the village freely, sniffing tobacco like a man, discussing local politics and talking back with biting wit. These were people, not walking ideologies. There was an ideology of gender inequality not unlike that in many feudal societies. A man was supposed to be able to control the women of his family. If he could not, if other men could look at them, tease them or have sex with them, he ate shame. Shame was dangerous for the whole family. A man without honour was a man who could not defend himself. And when a man could not defend himself or his family then powerful men would come and take his land or his sheep. The whole family would be left with nothing. So every one tried to claim they were honourable. But in practice the gender ideology of honour and shame punished poor men and poor women together.

Women were not men's equals in 1972. But they were not medieval slaves. One of the greatest virtues of the Communists, men and women, was that they wanted women's liberation. The Communists had women activists, women fighters with guns and women in government. They saw that the oppression of women was part and parcel of the exploitation and oppression that permeated all of Afghan society. Yet they ended up bombing women and children alongside their men.

Through the Communists, the liberation of women became identified with the torturers, the invaders, the helicopter gunships and the napalm. That is the logic which allows the Taliban today to identify beating unveiled women in the cities with opposition to imperialism.

None of this is to deny that the Taliban are reactionary. They are enemies of most women, as they are enemies of most ordinary Afghan people. But their ideas are not traditional, essentially Afghan or Pashtun. In the eyes of most Muslims they are a repellent, heretical interpretation of Islam. Their ideas are new, the product of 20 years of war, betrayal and suffering.

Many of the ideas the Taliban learned in the religious schools came from Saudi Arabia. Saudi is not some backwater. It is at the centre of world capitalism. The US government and the oil corporations have always been the allies and masters of the Saudi royal family. The ideology of the Saudi royal family, too, is one of oppressing women in the name of Islam. The Saudi princes talk of forbidding drink, amputating the hands of thieves and punishing the immodesty of women. Then they go to Beirut, Bahrain, Cairo and London to use prostitutes and drink themselves into stupors. They steal the public purse blind, export the money to London, and yet every Saudi prince still has both hands. The worse their corruption and lying, the more the Saudi people hate them. And the more they are hated, the more hypocritical and vicious they become in their prating about what they imagine Islam to be.

In Kabul, a police unit called the Society for the Propagation of Virtue and the Suppression of Vice patrols the streets and beats women who are 'improperly dressed'. In Saudi a police unit called the Society for the Propagation of Virtue and the Oppression of Vice has long done the same. And yet we do not see Tony Blair on our TV screens calling for women's rights in Saudi Arabia. Nor does George Bush call for elections and freedom there. The Saudi state keeps the oil safe for US corporations. What is revolting about the Taliban comes not from Afghan tradition, but from the needs and deeds of the centre of the world system.

In 2000 the Taliban controlled most of Afghanistan. The US had turned decisively against them, and so, more recently, had the Saudis. The reason was Osama Bin Laden, once the CIA's man in the Afghan resistance. When the Russians left, Bin Laden went home to Saudi Arabia, some say appalled by the corruption and faction fighting of the Islamists. There the Gulf War turned him against the Saudi government. Bin Laden approved of the US and Saudi alliance against Iraq. What he could not stomach was the stationing of US planes and troops in Saudi Arabia after the Gulf War. Everyone in Saudi, not just Bin Laden, knew the US forces remained in case the Saudi people rose against their rulers.

He had fought the Western (Russian) occupation in Afghanistan. Now the US was occupying his own country, the land of the holy places. He made the connection between the Russian bombing of Afghanistan and the US bombing of Iraq.

Because Bin Laden was a rich man, because he was right wing, and because he did not believe that ordinary people could or should rule the world, Bin Laden identified the people of the US with their government. It was the same mistake that many Americans have made recently, believing that the ordinary people of Afghanistan should suffer for the sins of the dictators who oppress them.

Bin Laden took refuge first in Sudan, and then in Afghanistan. There the Taliban welcomed him as an old comrade from the war. From there he led his organisation, now directed against US power and its Saudi clients. It still had the old name it had had when the US paid and ran him—al-Qaida. Now it was an embarrassment, and a danger, for the Saudi royal family. The US asked the Taliban to turn over Bin Laden. The Taliban said they would only do it through a proper extradition process, and the US would have to present evidence. The US government refused, perhaps because it did not have the evidence, but more likely because it did not recognise the Taliban. In any case, the Taliban could not turn him over. Their whole legitimacy, such as it was, relied upon being more Muslim than thou. If they turned over Bin Laden they would lose what support they had.

Then came 11 September in New York and at the Pentagon. Bin Laden praised that. I don't know if he personally organised it or not. But that was not really the point. US imperial power had been grievously wounded. The attack on the World Trade Centre was a blow. The easy destruction of part of the Pentagon, that home and symbol of US military might, was a worse blow to imperial power. And it was seen around the world before it disappeared from media sight. There are large parts of the Middle East that Washington dominates only through fear. If US power looks weak, the ugly dictatorships there may defy it. More seriously, the workers in the cities might rise up and take control of the oil from the US corporations. And most Muslims in the world live in cities.

The first instinct of Bush, Cheney and Powell was that US power had to be stamped on the Middle East anew. The terrorists, all of them, all over the Middle East, had to be hunted down like animals. Something had to be done so crushing that the humiliation of the Pentagon would be forgotten.

They found out soon enough that an attack on Iraq, Lebanon or Hamas in Israel would light a fire in the Arab world they might never put out. So they turned to the weakest, least defended, most friendless and desperate place they could find to punish—Afghanistan.

Even there US power seems ringed by constraints. The Pakistani, Saudi or Egyptian governments might at any moment withdraw from the US coalition. More serious yet, the people of Karachi or Riyadh or Cairo might rise up and forbid the killing in Afghanistan. So the US government treads warily.

At first the Northern Alliance commanders welcomed the prospect of US bombing of the Taliban-controlled cities that would enable them to sweep to Kabul. Nothing could expose more clearly the shame and venality of the people who lead the Northern Alliance. But the US forbade the Northern Alliance to advance on Kabul. India backed the Northern Alliance, and Colin Powell had promised the military dictatorship of Pakistan that only allies of Pakistan would hold Kabul. And there was still the oil of Central Asia. Iran and Russia now backed the Northern Alliance. The American government had no intention of letting them hold the road to Turkmenistan, Uzbekistan and oil.

Pakistani Inter Services Intelligence promised the US it would buy the support of warlords and some Taliban leaders and construct a new government. It found it could not.

With no other policy, the US government did what it knew how to do. It bombed. The US government said it was attacking only military targets, in a country where many soldiers are just men in turbans with a gun who live with their families. It dropped cluster bombs. It bombed the radio station in Kabul in the first few days. And, as always, civilians died. As I write, the civilian death toll is over 1,500, and the carpet-bombing has begun. The serious demolition of Kandahar and Herat is in progress. Many Taliban soldiers are dead too. I do not hold with the view that it is wrong to kill civilians but alright to kill soldiers. Many of the Taliban soldiers are boys and young men, the product of 20 years of refugee camps and war. Many are conscripts. Like the civilians, they are victims of history and vengeance.

The death toll in Afghanistan has now more or less reached that in New York. I was born in New York and have lived in Afghanistan. I've seen people cry for their dead in both countries. The pain looks the same. Yet there is one difference—the Afghans have had 23 years of war. Thirty years ago many Afghans put their faith in the Communists, and were utterly betrayed. Then many put their faith in the Islamists, and were betrayed again. Some of those who could still hope hoped the Taliban would be better, and were betrayed again.

They have lost over 1 million dead in those wars, perhaps another million maimed by bombs. Again, as in 1972, there is the threat of famine. In three years of drought many of the nomads have lost their animals. This time, unlike 1972, they will starve in the eyes of the world. But this time the planes and the war machines will not allow the food through. The villagers are short of cash because last year the US government promised the Taliban subsidies and diplomatic recognition if they abolished opium growing. Trusting the US government, the Taliban banned poppies successfully. Now the grain harvest has failed, and many peasants have no cash to buy food. Meanwhile, opium production has increased massively in the areas controlled by the Northern Alliance. Most of it goes, of course, to the West. But it has also created an estimated 3 million heroin addicts in Pakistan, and a similar number in Iran.

The US government is serious about killing Bin Laden. But it is also pursuing the old imperialism. This is why it hesitates to let the Northern Alliance take Kabul. The Northern Alliance are backed by Iran and Russia. If they control Afghanistan they have influence over Central Asian oil and gas. That is also why there is no mention of democracy and elections for Afghanistan.

The US is thinking of restoring the old king, Zahir Shah, now 86 years old and in exile in Italy, to Kabul. He would rule through a *loya jirga*, literally a big tribal council. This was the old gathering of the feudal landlords. Now some new landlords, Islamists and 'moderate Taliban' would be added. The US government is aware this would be an imperial occupation. Afraid of the consequences elsewhere of occupying a Muslim state, they are looking to the Turkish army to take over. The Turkish army, it says, has plenty of relevant experience in Kurdistan. But only 17 percent of the population of Turkey support the US war. No plan anyone mentions includes free elections in Afghanistan. That would produce a government hostile to US and Pakistani power.

I was opposed to the revolution from above in 1978, and I still am. In an article written for this journal in 1981, I said that we had no choice but to support the resistance against the Russian invasion. In an article written in 1988, as the Russian army left, I said that after the invasion there was no party or group in Afghanistan that any decent person could support.[19] I stand by all of these positions. I do not mention these now to show that I am right—there is no consolation in that—but to show that the political tradition of Lenin, Trotsky, Rosa Luxemburg and this journal has always been opposed to revolution from above and to human liberation through helicopter gunships.

There will be no hope in the Middle East if the left there cannot understand that the Islamists now lead the resistance not because ordinary people are stupid or reactionary, but because the Islamists have seemed to be the only people fighting imperialism. The Islamists have served those people badly, and betrayed them when in power. But ordinary people can only be won from the Islamists by joining them in resistance to imperialism. This does not mean terrorism. That is another form of a small minority trying to impose their will on the world. It means mass demonstrations on the streets, and general strikes to back them up. This is now possible in several countries in the Middle East.

In Pakistan the Islamists now demonstrate carrying pictures of Bin Laden. The left demonstrates separately, carrying signs saying 'No to the Taliban, no to George Bush'. Both kinds of demonstrations are small. Ordinary workers in Pakistan do not by and large support the Islamists or the Taliban. But in their guts, day by day, they feel that George Bush is far more of an enemy than Mullah Omar. It would not be easy for the left and the Islamists to march together in Karachi. But if they did hundreds of thousands who support neither would fall in behind them.

It matters, too, what happens beyond the Middle East. The arguments about the way to human liberation always happen around the world. The Communists in Afghanistan made the mistakes they did because the ideas of revolution from above, of socialism as dictatorship, were the dominant ideas among revolutionaries over most of the world. The Soviet Union is gone now, and with that there is a space to build a new democratic socialist revolutionary movement.

These are dark times. Our world is full of the maimed and grieving from many wars. But there is an alternative, and it is not abstract. There is a movement against this war, on the streets of Quetta, Lahore, Peshawar, Oman, Bethlehem, London, Calcutta, Rome, Berlin, Jakarta, and in the last month on the streets of New York, Washington, and 200 other US cities. No peace movement before has ever grown so large, so quickly. Millions have demonstrated. In the West the peace movement expresses the views of tens of millions. In the Middle East we are the majority. Like the anti-capitalist movement, this one is international and internationalist. Millions are learning hand over fist how the world system works and how ordinary people can resist. We need to find the other people in that movement who want to change the world, and bring them together.

So far the ordinary people in Mazar, Jalalabad and across Afghanistan have not given in to the bombers. They may break yet. Every dream they fought for has turned to blood, torture and theft. They have seen 23 years of war, more than 1 million dead and perhaps 1 million maimed, and they face famine. But with no leaders they can trust or respect, they have not yet given in to the terror from the skies. That courage gives me hope for the rest of us.

'The land of the Afghans, the land of tyrants,' the patient in the TB hospital said, and we all gave an angry laugh. The tyrants are worse now.

There has been no lack of dreams and idealism in Afghanistan these last 30 years. Ordinary Afghans, both Communists and Mujahadeen, have fought with great courage over many years. Their leaders have betrayed their ideals utterly. Worse than that have been the outside powers that have played the Great Game with the arms and legs and skulls of Afghans.

They, the rulers of Russia and the US, but also Pakistan, Saudi Arabia, India, Iran, Uzbekistan and now Britain, are the true tyrants. They have taken a poor and desperate place, and made it a hell.

Bush and Blair are cruel men, without shame. It is time we had a world where no one ever again spends $10 million to incinerate a child.

Notes

1   The analysis of Afghan history in this article is set out in more detail in J Neale, 'The Afghan Tragedy', *International Socialism* 12 (Spring 1981), and J Neale, 'Afghanistan: The Horse Changes Riders', *Capital and Class* 35 (1998).

2   I use feudal not in the narrow European and Japanese sense of a system of feudal allegiance and a tied peasantry. I use it in the more general sense of a social system where national power lies in the hands of large landowners who live in the countryside. In this sense, Afghanistan and Ethiopia in the 1970s were the last two feudal countries, and now there are none.

3   Two books by Barnett Rubin are very useful on the importance of subsidies from abroad: *The Fragmentation of Afghanistan: State Formation and Collapse in the International System* (New Haven, 1995), and *The Search for Peace in Afghanistan* (New Haven, 1995).

4   The best books on Afghan history from 1838 to 1929 are J Kaye, *History of the War in Afghanistan* (London, 1878), still one of the masterpieces of the historian's art; C Masson, *Narrative of Various Journeys* (London, 1842); J Norris, *The First Afghan War, 1838-1842* (Cambridge, 1967); S Mohammed, *The Life of the Amir Abdul Rahman* (London, 1900); M H Kakar, *Afghanistan: A Study in Internal Political Developments, 1880-1896* (Kabul, 1971); L Poullada, *Reform and Rebellion in Afghanistan, 1919-1929* (Ithica, 1973); V Gregorian, *The Emergence of Modern Afghanistan: Politics of Reform and Modernization 1880-1946* (Stanford, 1969); D Edwards, *Heroes of the Age: Moral Fault Lines on the Afghan Frontier* (Berkeley, 1996).

5   For the ways in which the regime systematically thwarted economic development see M Fry, *The Afghan Economy* (Leiden, 1974).

6   For Afghan Islamists the best source is O Roy, *Islam and Resistance in Afghanistan* (Cambridge, 1986).

7   M Barry, *Afghanistan* (Paris, 1974).

8   The best account of Afghan Communism in these years is R Anwar, *The Tragedy of Afghanistan* (London, 1988). Anwar, a Pakistani, was a socialist political prisoner in Kabul in the 1980s. Many dissident Communists talked openly with him because lies no longer mattered. A good account from the point of view of the US government is H Bradshaw, *Afghanistan and the Soviet Union* (Durham, NC, 1985).

9   That is to say, most people in Central Asia belonged to ethnic groups that had once been overwhelmingly Muslim. In 1980 they were, by and large, not active worshippers, and many were not believers, but the possibility of organising politically under the banner of Islam remained.

10   There is a good account of this in the very useful book by M H Kakar, *Afghanistan: The Soviet Invasion and the Afghan Response, 1979-1982* (Berkeley, 1995). Kakar is sometimes a Pashtun chauvinist, but an honest and very well informed man.

11   The best sources on the Mujahadeen inside Afghanistan are A Bonner, *Among the Afghans* (Durham, NC, 1987), and O Roy, op cit.

12   This is taken from my own field research. For an excellent account of the system of *qaums* in another part of Afghanistan before the war, see R Canfield, 'Faction and Conversion in a Plural Society: Religious Alignments in the Hindu Kush', University of Michigan Museum of Anthropology Papers 50 (1973).

13   I know of two exceptions to this localism. In the long valley of Panjshir, north of Kabul, the Islamist leader Ahmed Shah Massoud was able to unite the whole region into one *qaum*, and sometimes able to lead his fighters out of the valley towards the road from Kabul to the north. And in the mountains in the centre of the country, it seems that the Hazara people were for a time able to combine into one force. But in general there were only small local groups.

14   On the CIA and drugs in many places, see A McCoy, *The Politics of Heroin: CIA Complicity in the Global Drugs Trade* (New York, 1991). For an interesting discussion of why drugs and covert war so often go together, see R Naylor, *Hot Money and the Politics of Debt* (London, 1987).

15   For Bin Laden see particularly Michael Griffin, *Reaping the Whirlwind: The Taliban Movement in Afghanistan* (London, 2001). J Cooley, *Unholy Wars: Afghanistan, America and International Terrorism* (London, 2000) is also full of information, though his pro-imperialist and anti-Muslim sentiments can be irritating.

16   The best book on Afghanistan after 1988 is A Rashid, *Taliban: Islam, Oil and the New Great Game in Central Asia* (London, 2000). Also very useful is M Griffin, op cit, and the articles by Amin Saikal, Ahmed Rashid, Richard Mackenzie, Anthony Hyman, Anwar-ul-Haq, and especially Anthony Davis, 'How the Taliban Became a Military Force', all in W Maley (ed), *Fundamentalism Reborn? Afghanistan and the Taliban* (London, 1998).

17   There is some question about Babrak Karmal, who always said he was a Pashtun, but was regarded by many Pashtuns as belonging to another, Farsi-speaking, group.

18   The best book on the relationship between gender inequality and the more general system of inequality in Afghanistan is N Tapper, *Bartered Brides: Politics, Gender and Marriage in an Afghan Tribal Society* (Cambridge, 1991). Also very useful for thinking about gender in the Middle East more generally are, by the same author under a different surname, N Lindisfarne, 'Variant Masculinities, Variant Virginities: Rethinking "Honour and Shame"', in A Cornwall and N Lindisfarne (eds), *Dislocating Masculinity: Comparative Ethnographies* (London, 1994); and N Lindisfarne, *Thank God We're Secular* (Ankara, 2001). See also the very readable V Doubleday, *Three Women of Herat* (London, 1988).

19   See J Neale, 'The Afghan Tragedy', op cit; and J Neale, 'Afghanistan: The Horse Changes Riders', op cit.

The next issue of **Revolutionary History** on the themes of mutiny, armies and revolutionary agitation is out soon.

Contents

◆ *Mutiny and the Cohesion of the Armed Services*, Ted Crawford
◆ *The Enigma of Kersausie: Engels In June 1848*, Ian Birchall
◆ *Marxism and the Problems of War* [1914], Karl Radek
◆ *The Origins of the Potemkin Revolt* [1905], Anatoli Petrovich Berezovsky
◆ *1917—The Revolt of the Russian Soldiers in France/The Bolshevik Revolution Seen Through the Eyes of the Soldiers of the Russian Expeditionary Corps In France*, Rémi Adam
◆ *The Revolt at Radomir*, Tico Jossifort, Boian Kostelov
◆ *The Black Sea Revolt*, written with the assistance of three participants in the mutinies, Marcel Monribot, Charles Tillon and Virgile Vuillemin.
◆ *Negotiations at Simla, India in 1919*
◆ Sir Basil Thomson's *Report on Revolutionary Organisations in the United Kingdom* [4.11.1920] with the text of the likely faked British Red Army 'Red Officers' Course'
◆ *Comintern Work in the Armed Forces of the West in the 1930s*, David McKnight
◆ *Work in the Army*, Comintern Report [10.10.1935], Boris Vasilyev
◆ Interview with YCL activist Dave Wallis—*Wivenhoe, Cairo: Eighth Army, World War II*
◆ *Defiance in the Ranks: British Trotskyists in Egypt 1944-1946*, David Renton
◆ Interview with Duncan Hallas—*Memories of Mutiny in Egypt in 1946*

Plus Introductions, Bibliographies and Notes by Esther Leslie, Julian Putkowski, John Plant and others.
The issue also includes other materials including Obituaries, Reports on Work in Progress, Reviews, Letters and Readers' Notes.

Likely price—£9.95: Please enquire for confirmation of price. To order a copy contact Barry Buitekant at barry.buitekant@tesco.net or write to him at Socialist Platform Ltd, BCM 7646, London WC1N 3XX, England.

Cheques should be made payable to 'Socialist Platform Ltd'.
Credit Card enquiries to Barry are also welcome.
In London, the journal is available at Porcupine Bookcellar, 5 Caledonian Road, London N1 9DX (tel: 020 7837 4473).

The crisis in the Middle East

ANNE ALEXANDER

As US and British fighter jets screamed across Afghan skies during the Afghan war, many people in the Middle East will have seen a mirror image of their own experiences of the past decade. In the villages of the West Bank they know what it is like to wake up night after night to the sound of helicopter gunships pounding the neighbourhood with rockets. In the dusty, impoverished towns of Iraq, they know too well the terror of cruise missile strikes, and the reality of saturation bombing. Both Iraqis and Palestinians have experienced the slower but equally lethal effects of economic blockade. The Western powers recognise that high technology warfare is at its most deadly when combined with the ancient brutality of siege and starvation.

In the 11 years since the end of the Gulf War the US has suffered no serious challenge to its domination of the Middle East. Neither local states nor regional rivals have yet threatened the 'New World Order' constructed by George Bush Sr. and now defended by his son. Russian president Vladimir Putin gave his support for the launch of air attacks on Afghanistan, even though, according to Israeli television reports, George Bush called Israeli prime minister Ariel Sharon an hour before he rang the Kremlin.[1] After Israeli forces stormed the Haram al-Sharif and slaughtered protesters at the Al-Aqsa mosque[2] in Jerusalem last year, triggering a new intifada, the Arab regimes could only offer reluctant verbal support for the Palestinians.

Yet the war on Afghanistan has only sharpened the underlying contradictions on which US policy in the Middle East is based. The leaders of the Arab world are walking a tightrope between the demands of their patrons in Washington and pressure from their own peoples. This conflict is not simply a result of popular anger at the humiliation of Palestine and Iraq, it is also a result of the contradictions produced by the programmes of economic liberalisation which the US has demanded as part of the price for its patronage.

It is no accident that the key figures in Osama Bin Laden's organisation, al-Qaida, are from Egypt and Saudi Arabia, the most important Arab supporters of the US.[3] In Egypt—the first country in the Middle East to begin a programme of economic liberalisation—'structural adjustment' has been a painful process for ordinary people. Living standards have been falling for more than a generation. Hosni Mubarak's regime relies on a brutal security apparatus to stifle dissent. The Saudi economy has also been in crisis for more than a decade. Since the early 1980s per capita income has collapsed from $16,000 per year to less than $7,000.[4] Economic crisis and the demands of the US sap the political legitimacy of both regimes. It is a measure of the bankruptcy of the leaders of the Arab world that both the secular nationalist regimes which came out of the great liberation movements of the 1940s and the conservative religious states of the Gulf are equally dependent on American favour.

However, it is also a measure of the weakness of even the Islamist opposition that neither Osama Bin Laden nor the Egyptian Islamist Ahmad al-Zawahiri, described by the media as Bin Laden's 'right hand man',[5] have so far had much success in destabilising their own governments. Ironically, US intervention in Afghanistan has the potential to achieve this more quickly than years of underground work in Egypt or Saudi Arabia ever did. In addition, groups such as al-Qaida will not automatically benefit from the crisis. The current hysteria in the West over 'Islamic terrorism' obscures the fact that recent history in the region is full of the failures of Islamist groups to relate to the mass movements they have unleashed. Islamist organisations which have successfully seized state power represent a tiny fraction of the movement as a whole.

This article attempts to map out the contradictions of US policy in the Middle East, and the shaky foundations on which the war in Afghanistan depends. It also examines the economic forces shaping the crisis of imperialism in the region, and discusses the potential for resistance from the nationalist movements, the Islamists and the working class.

The price of imperial power

The crisis in the Middle East is the product of pressure on the region at two levels—firstly through the direct intervention of the great powers, in particular the US, and by the actions of its local clients. The second driving force behind the crisis is the economic pressure created by the imposition of free market policies at the urging of the World Bank and the IMF. The close relationship between economic and military intervention in the Middle East shows that Lenin's theory of imperialism is as relevant as ever. In 1915 he described how war was built into the logic of the capitalist system, as economic rivalry spilled over into military competition.[6] The intense competition between the rival great powers over the resources of the Middle East, particularly the region's oil and gas, has guaranteed a century of conflict. At times the great powers have been content to control the area from a distance, through their local client states. For instance, Israel has consciously played a role as the guarantor of European and American interests in the Middle East for more than 50 years.[7]

However, over the past decade the US has increasingly been pulled into direct military action, either with its own forces, or under the cover of the United Nations. At the same time, the impact of what millions now recognise as 'globalisation' is just as sharply felt in the Middle East as it is in Asia, Europe or the Americas. The interaction between globalisation and imperialism is creating a crisis in the region which US bombing can only intensify. Imperialism is not a static system. In fact, the opposite is true. Over the last decade we have witnessed an escalating cycle of war and instability across the globe. Each time the US government has taken military action to defend its interests, it has left behind wrecked economies, shattered countries and generations of bitter survivors. Proving the superiority of American weaponry on the broken bodies of Afghan civilians will not produce any kind of durable basis for US control of the Middle East.

It is the US's relationship with the Arab regimes which has come under the most pressure over the past few years. Through a mixture of selective bribery and thinly disguised threats the US has maintained the support of the Arab governments of the Middle East. Despite loud calls for action over the intifada, the Arab rulers have in most cases gone no further than rhetorical support. Palestinian planning minister Nabil Sha'ath complained in March that only $3 million out of a $1 billion fund promised to the Palestinian Authority at the Arab Summit the previous year had been paid out.[8] Most of the Arab regimes have been willing for US planes to use their airstrips and US warships to pass through their ports. In return, these governments have armed themselves from US stock, and gained access to international credit with the 'bankers of last resort' at the IMF. Yet all this has come at a heavy price. The presence of US troops in the Arabian peninsula is a source of shame for many Saudis. A large number of Americans have died in a bombing campaign carried out by opposition groups opposed to US use of Saudi bases.[9] Nearly 20 US sailors died in a suicide attack on the *USS Cole* at harbour in the Yemeni port of Aden.[10] Even Oman, which has little history of large-scale protest, witnessed angry demonstrations against the US and British bombing of Afghanistan at the same time as thousands of British troops were taking part in military exercises there.[11]

There is a relentless dynamic to all this process. Imperialist direct intervention undermines the US's local allies and increases the instability in the region. Instead of pulling the strings from a distance, the US is forced increasingly to commit troops and vast amounts of military hardware to maintaining its power. Yet that very military action, although usually successful in dealing with the immediate threat to US interests, in the long term puts more pressure on the US's local clients. Thus the need to subdue Iraq has led to the permanent presence of US warplanes on Saudi soil, and thus a permanent source of resentment for a significant layer of Saudi society.

Likewise, the US's reliance on Israel has its price. Every incursion into the West Bank, every 12 year old stone thrower shot dead, every house demolition, adds to the resentment ordinary people across the Middle East feel against the US, Israel and their own rulers. The pressures building up inside Israeli society which led to the election of Ariel Sharon have been one of the driving forces behind the brutality of Israel's response to the intifada. Sharon gives expression to the voice of that section within Israeli society which favours a military solution to the Palestinian 'problem'. The far right minister of tourism, Rehavam Ze'evi, who was shot dead by the Popular Front for the Liberation of Palestine in October, was one of the most vocal advocates of the policy of 'transfer'—a euphemism for the mass expulsion of the Palestinians from Israel and the Occupied Territories.[12] As the contradictions within Israeli society have grown, the right wing has been able to exercise more and more control over the direction of Israeli policy. The Oslo peace process was essentially the work of the Israeli Labour Party. The collapse of the peace deals means that achieving the settlement the US so badly needs will be extremely difficult. This is not least because, as the ongoing intifada demonstrates, Palestinians are no longer prepared to make concessions for empty promises.

The devastation caused by the US-led war on Iraq must rank as one of the great crimes of the 20th century. The figures are a testimony to horror on an unimaginable scale. According to the United Nations 500,000 Iraqi children have died as a result of the sanctions regime.[13] Another 500,000 children have developed cancer, which many scientists believe is a legacy of the depleted uranium weapons used during the war.[14]

Confronted by these figures on the prime-time US news programme *60 Minutes*, Madeleine Albright, then US ambassador to the United Nations, hardly hesitated before replying, 'I think this is a very hard choice, but the price—we think the price is worth it'.[15]

In political and military terms, the first few years after the US victory seemed to have proved her right. The destruction of Iraq served as a suitable reminder to friends and enemies alike of the power of the US military. The Gulf War was crucial in pushing a number of states towards an accommodation with the US, particularly those such as Syria, which found themselves without superpower patrons after the collapse of the Soviet Union. US success in the Gulf War also brought significant military advantages:

> *US troops, planes and weapons stand ready at bases in Saudi Arabia, Turkey and elsewhere in the region, and the US Navy's Sixth Fleet prowls the Gulf on virtually permanent assignment. Stationing US military forces in the Gulf was one of Washington's biggest prizes from the war. Even the truck-bomb attack on the Khobar Towers barracks in Saudi Arabia, which killed dozens of US service personnel, did not lead to troop withdrawals. They are in the Gulf for the long haul.*[16]

Despite this the US has also paid a price for its victory. Since 1991 the international coalition which supported US military action has slowly began to unravel. The sheer vindictiveness of the sanctions regime has eroded public support for the siege against Iraq. Madeleine Albright could not speak in public without being met by anti-sanctions protesters. France, Russia and China abstained on the motion to the UN Security Council renewing the sanctions regime in 1999.[17] UN officials Denis Halliday, Hans von Sponeck and Jutta Burghardt all resigned from high-level posts in protest at what Halliday described as the 'genocidal impact' of sanctions.[18] By 1999 the *Wall Street Journal* commented that it was now 'unclear which side was more isolated: the dictator who has successfully defied sanctions, or the Anglo-US alliance that insists they remain in place'.[19]

In addition the presence of US troops on Saudi soil provides a rallying call for the radical Saudi opposition. A series of devastating bomb attacks, including the huge truck bomb at the Khobar Towers base near Dhahran, have targeted US military and civilian personnel.[20] The latest attack on al-Khobar city on 6 October killed two US soldiers.[21] Foreign troops are not simply an affront to national pride for Saudi patriots. More seriously, for a regime which legitimates itself on religious grounds, the Saudi opposition can draw on a long tradition of Islamic thought to argue that the US bases are tantamount to blasphemy. Important figures from the religious opposition gave a fatwa, or religious judgement, excommunicating the

Saudi royal family from Islam for supporting the US onslaught on Afghanistan.[22] The demand for US withdrawal from Saudi Arabia is a key element of Osama Bin Laden's campaign against the Saudi royal family. In 1996 he issued this call for action:

> The presence of the US crusader forces in Muslim Gulf states...is the greatest danger and poses the most serious harm, threatening the world's largest oil reserves. The ordinary Saudi knows that his country is the largest oil producer in the world, yet at the same time he is suffering from taxes and bad services. Our country has become a colony of America. The Saudis know their real enemy is America.[23]

Dilip Hiro argued recently in *Middle East International* that some defence analysts see the potential internal threat to the Saudi regime as the primary reason for basing thousands of troops there. In the case of an armed uprising against the Saudi royal family, 'the presence of US military officials at key Saudi defence facilities, often in civilian clothes...is regarded as indispensable in order to ensure swift co-ordination and secure communications in such an emergency'.[24]

The end of the oil sheikhs?

The corrosion of the royal family's religious legitimacy is not the only factor driving the crisis in Saudi Arabia. Until recently the Saudi ruling class was able to buy the obedience of the majority of the native population. Saudi Arabia is home to 25 percent of the world's known reserves of crude oil.[25] Oil created fabulous wealth for the Saudi royal family and turned a small, poor country into a regional power. It also created a permanent connection between the interests of the Saudi rulers and their political patrons in the US. A joint venture between the US oil companies and the US government during the Second World War laid the ground for the explosion in Saudi oil production.[26] In 1938 Saudi oilfields were producing only 0.1 million tonnes of crude per year, but by 1955 that had risen to 47.5 million tonnes.[27] Oil revenues powered the entire Saudi economy, fuelling a huge construction boom as the petrodollars took shape as airports, highways, offices and palaces for the Saudi elite. The royal family allowed no space for democratic debate, but Saudi citizens enjoyed a high standard of living in return for their silence. Healthcare, education and generous state subsidies in the form of well paid jobs in the government bureaucracy cemented ordinary Saudis to the ruling class.[28]

Naturally this privilege has always been exercised at the expense of millions of non-citizens who have formed a permanent layer of misery in Saudi society. Menial jobs as labourers, cleaners and nannies have traditionally been reserved for workers from India, South East Asia and other Arab states. These workers have long been considered expendable by the Saudi ruling class—trade unions are illegal, strikes are banned and activists can easily be deported.[29] However, over the last few years this distinction has begun to break down as more and more Saudi citizens have been forced into unskilled, low paid work by the growing economic crisis. The first factor in this process has been the volatility of the oil sector itself. Over the last 20 years oil prices have on average been low compared to the 1970s. Partly this is a result of the last world economic crisis, which has prevented oil consumption from reaching the level of the late 1970s.[30] Combined with other factors such as the oil cartel OPEC's decision to recapture market share by increasing production, this led to overproduction on a grand scale. According to the International Energy Agency, despite relatively high prices world supply of oil is currently exceeding demand by around 1 million barrels per day.[31] As the US economy slides further into crisis, this excess is likely to increase. Any country which depends on a single commodity, even one so precious as oil, is particularly vulnerable in a global recession. Nearly 90 percent of the Saudi government's revenues for 2000 came from the oil sector.[32]

The underlying problems in the Saudi economy are compounded by the schizophrenia in Saudi society. Prestige projects from a generation ago still look impressive on publicity photographs for investment brochures, but they hide the reality of a basic social infrastructure which often barely functions. Most Saudi cities suffer regular power cuts and water rationing. Jedda, a port with 3 million inhabitants, has 300 palaces but no sewage system. A population explosion over the last 30 years means that around 100,000 young Saudis are entering the labour market each year. Currently there are only jobs available for around half that number.[33] Officially, unemployment is running at around 18 percent, but the real figure is probably much higher among young graduates. At the same time average income has collapsed. Across the Middle East millions of people live with the gnawing fear that they will never reach the modest standard of living that their parents enjoyed. For young Saudis, the sudden closing down of their horizons has been acutely painful. *Jane's Sentinel* defence risk assessments gave this stark analysis of the potential for instability within Saudi society in May 2001:

> *While the population growth rate exceeds the economic growth rate, the mounting unemployment and resultant disaffected youth increases the potential for instability. Moreover, the exponential growth of the royal family—that numbers in the tens of thousands—is also draining the economy and may compel the inner royal family to curb royal allowances. This could create another disaffected section in Saudi society.*[34]

For the Saudi ruling class, the answer to the problem of unemployment is straightforward: 'We don't, in the government of Saudi Arabia, admit there is unemployment, basically because there are the jobs... There are 6 or 7 million expatriates working in the kingdom. Many of those jobs can be done by Saudis'.[35] Creating a native Saudi working class may ease the pressure on government stipends, but it clearly involves other dangers for the ruling class. In a society which is rigidly ruled from above, there are almost no legal outlets for the frustration of the younger generation. It is at this level where economic resentment grates on the kingdom's relationship with the imperialist powers. For the time being this is confined to marginal opposition groups which offer a religious critique of the existing regime. As the Saudi working class continues to grow, this has the potential to develop into a force which can give a real social base to the Saudi opposition.

The revenge of the market

The other side of US control of the Middle East is through the financial institutions. Across the region economic problems have heightened social tensions and left the rulers of the region walking a tightrope between the demands of the international financial institutions and the growing frustration from below. So far they have succeeded in maintaining their balance, but, as in Saudi Arabia, the political instability created by imperialist intervention always threatens to push one or more of the Arab regimes over the brink. In every country the pace of privatisation and economic reform is accelerating. In Egypt, although the actual process has been slow, the cumulative effect of years of free market reforms has eaten away at support for the regime.

By contrast, in a number of other countries, such as Lebanon, Iran and Syria, the effects of economic liberalisation have so far been contradictory. In all these countries a section of the ruling class has been able to link the idea of free market reform with the hope of political liberalisation. In Iran and Syria this is a reflection of debates within the ruling class itself about how to reform without losing control of the process. The Iranian economy has benefited from the high oil prices of the past few years, thus allowing the 'reformists' grouped around President Mohammed Khatami a chance to continue the process of liberalisation.[36] In Syria power passed smoothly from Hafez al-Asad to his son Bashar, who briefly allowed political meetings and discussion groups to start meeting for the first time in years. However, both the limited Iranian political liberalisation and the brief 'Syrian spring' are based on shaky foundations. As the world economy tips further into recession, oil prices are likely to fall, raising the pressure on the Iranian economy. Prices in

Iran are still rising sharply—the consumer goods price index for July-August 2001 was up 11.8 percent. In recent years there have been huge numbers of demonstrations in protest at rising unemployment, lack of basic services and public transport.[37] Bashar al-Asad's toleration of dissent lasted only a few months after the death of his father—the discussion groups have been shut down and opposition leaders sent back to prison. Riyad al-Turk, the leader of the Syrian Communist Party, was returned to jail at the end of August 2001 for writing an article criticising Hafez al-Asad for turning Syria into 'a hereditary republic'.[38]

In Lebanon privatisation is presented as the way to rid the country of religious sectarianism. Elsewhere old fashioned ideas of state control are blamed for overstaffed and inefficient public sector companies. The Lebanese ruling class, by contrast, has consciously raised the spectre of a return to the horrors of civil war in the debate on privatisation. Under the leadership of Rafiq Hariri, 'Lebanon's Berlusconi', the government has begun a sweeping programme of privatisation.[39] Plans to privatise the electricity supply, fixed-line telephone services and other state firms were drawn up in March 2001.[40] When the government picked out Middle East Airlines, Lebanon's national carrier, for 1,200 job losses workers' anger erupted:

On June 21, employees of the Lebanese national carrier Middle East Airlines (MEA) attacked company headquarters and staged demonstrations, after being informed by MEA management of the imminent layoff of 1,200 workers in preparation for the airline's scheduled privatisation. Top administrators, including the company's director-general, Mohammed Hout, were kept locked in their offices by angry employees.[41]

Although the strike, which was led by the Shi'ite guerrilla organisation Hizbollah, was eventually defeated, it is clear that, so long as they are expected to bear the costs of liberalisation, workers in Lebanon will rapidly come to hate privatisation as much as their Egyptian counterparts.

Workers in countries which have started to privatise relatively late have only to look to Egypt to see a likely vision of their future. Egypt was the first of the Arab regimes to open up to Western economic patronage. Anwar al-Sadat's policy of 'infitah', or economic liberalisation, in the 1970s gave a range of incentives to direct foreign investment. Sadat also went to the IMF for a loan, only to be told that the price would be the abolition of subsidies on basic foodstuffs. Egyptians woke up one morning in January 1977 to find that the price of flour, sugar, kerosene and bread had risen by 22 percent.[42] A spontaneous urban uprising on a scale not seen in Egypt since the revolution of 1919 forced a panicky Sadat to reinstate the subsidies. Since that date Egyptian governments have been forced to make their cuts more subtly in the fear that other drastic measures could spark another revolt.

In reality, despite a temporary respite for the last few years of Sadat's rule, the economic pressure on ordinary Egyptians has not slackened for the last 20 years. The social value of wages has fallen continuously, often as a result of the loss of so called 'fringe benefits' which both private and state companies are eliminating in the name of market efficiency. These production bonuses, protected pensions and overtime payments are often all that keeps families out of absolute poverty.[43] The introduction of free market rents into the already desperately overcrowded housing sector has added to the financial pressure.[44] In addition the public health and education systems are approaching collapse after years of degradation. Thus the only way to pass crucial high school and university exams is by paying for the expensive private tutorials which teachers offer to eke out their meagre salaries.

The countryside has felt the impact of market reforms even more harshly. While poor urban families in 1997 spent a staggering 57.9 percent of their income on food, that rose to 63.4 percent for their counterparts in Egypt's villages. Even more revealing is the percentage of food expenditure which was used to purchase just bread, cooking oil and sugar. Among the urban poor these three basic goods accounted for 35.4 percent of food expenditure while in rural areas that rose to 40.3 percent.[45] Land reforms which abolished the limit on landholding size and removed the ceiling on agricultural rents have had a catastrophic effect on tenant farmers. According to the Land Centre for Human Rights, around 700,000 tenant farmers have lost out since the reforms came into effect in 1997. In one year alone the average rent increased five fold from £E120 per feddan to £E660.[46] Even the *Financial Times* was blunt about the impact of the land reforms. 'The reversion to pre-Nasserite agrarian capitalism has been abrupt'.[47]

Throughout the 1990s the IMF and the Egyptian government pointed to the 'transformation' of the Egyptian economy by the structural adjustment programmes. Financial reforms following the severe economic crisis and the collapse of the Egyptian pound in the currency markets in 1990 supposedly paved the way for a new era of growth. In fact, as Tim Mitchell explains in *Middle East Report*, the financial reforms 'were not so much an elimination of state support (as the neo-liberal version would have it), but rather, a change in recipients'.[48] The state intervened in the financial markets to bail out the banks and underwrite a massive expansion in private sector lending which has fuelled an immense speculative building boom. This has benefited the handful of private companies which are large enough to take advantage of the loans. Many of these hold the local franchise for some of the most powerful multinationals on the planet, such as McDonald's, Philips and Microsoft. These Egyptian corporations have used the leverage provided by the state at the behest of the IMF and the World Bank to launch themselves into the global marketplace:

> These conglomerates produce goods and services affordable to just a small fraction of Egypt's population. A meal at McDonald's costs more than most workers earn in a day... The Ahram Beverages Company, which makes soft drinks, bottled water and beer, calculates its potential market (including expatriates and tourists) to be just five or six million, in a country of 62 million. This narrow market corresponds to that segment of the population that can afford, or even imagine affording, the country's one million private cars—which is why local manufacturers concentrate on assembling Mercedes, BMWs, Jeep Cherokees and other luxury cars.[49]

Globalisation for the Middle East means precisely this—a cartel, composed of the most powerful sections of local private capital, the upper layers of the state bureaucracy and the army, propelling itself into the second or third ranks of the global elite through the leverage of state intervention and the favour of the international financial institutions, while leaving the rest of the population to rot. Economic pressures have corroded the Arab rulers' domestic support to the point where it is hard to see any of the current regimes regaining the level of popular legitimacy they enjoyed a generation ago. Across the Middle East the intersection between local economic crisis and imperialist intervention has the potential to generate many further serious confrontations between the local and global ruling classes and the peoples of the region.

Between repression and revolt

It is clear that the objective conditions for a large-scale revolutionary crisis exist in a number of Middle Eastern countries. In addition to the combination of internal and external pressures on a large number of the US's allies,[50] the potential for linking mass movements across the existing national boundaries has never been greater. New media, in particular satellite television, have played an important role in generalising the intifada.[51]

Yet it is the subjective conditions which are ultimately crucial in turning riots into organised demonstrations, and street clashes with the police into a mass movement. In the Middle East over the past ten years two major currents have attempted to provide some kind of political leadership to the struggles of the people of the region. Firstly, the crisis in Palestine represents the unfinished business from the national liberation movements of the 1950s and 1960s. The renewed intifada, and the key role played by Fatah, the largest nationalist bloc in the PLO, demonstrate the lingering resonance of nationalist ideas. Secondly, the Islamist movement has responded to the crisis of imperialism with a kind of Muslim internationalism, which pits Islamist activists directly at the 'crusader' forces of imperialism.

Of all the conflicts in the Middle East, none symbolises the unequal struggle against imperialism better than the Palestinian intifada. The imagery of the intifada—children taking on tanks, the clashes in the streets of Gaza and the West Bank, the mass funerals and demonstrations —has been burned into the memories of a generation across the Middle East. For vast numbers of ordinary people, the impotence of the Arab regimes in the face of rising levels of brutality from the Israeli forces of occupation is just a mirror of their own humiliation.

Understanding how the intifada connects to the wider struggle in the Middle East is a vital part of grasping the real potential for resistance to Western imperialism and home-grown repression. Different political currents have all used not only the symbol of the intifada, but the actual techniques of popular uprising, in an attempt to generalise the struggle in Palestine across the Middle East. The weakness of the Palestinian bourgeoisie, and the completely overwhelming military and economic superiority of Israel have meant that the Palestinian national liberation movement has not yet succeeded in creating a state of its own. In many ways the experience of the Palestinian struggle is a testimony to the resilience of national liberation movements, as it is to the courage and creativity of ordinary Palestinian people. Yet the course of the intifada over the past year also shows the ultimate impotence of national struggle alone.

The underlying reason for this is simply the huge inequality between the two sides. Palestinian stone-throwers are facing the fourth largest military power on the planet, behind which stands the might of the greatest military power, the US. The scale of Israeli violence has been much greater than during the first uprising of 1987. This violence has been systematically applied since the very start of the uprising. A report by the respected Israeli human rights group B'Tselem on the events at the Haram al-Sharif after Ariel Sharon's visit there shows clear evidence that the Israeli army responded to a large, but mostly non-violent, protest with massive force.[52] The pattern of Palestinian deaths is also revealing. According to Palestinian sources, more than 200 children have been killed by Israeli troops during the last year. A very large proportion of these died as a result of wounds to the upper body or head, a clear indication that they were directly targeted, rather than simply falling victim to 'crossfire' as the Israelis have often claimed.[53] Beyond the hundreds killed, there are tens of thousands of Palestinians who have been permanently disabled by injuries received during the conflict. Given the meagre resources available to the Palestinian health system, and the crushing impact of economic blockades, these bald figures represent huge pools of misery for tens of thousands of Palestinians. The outbreak of the intifada has not stopped the flow of aid and arms from the US to Israel. In October 2000, only days after the massacre of Palestinians at the Al-Aqsa Mosque in Jerusalem, the Israeli Air Force concluded its largest ever deal with the US. This included the delivery of eight Apache combat helicopters as well as 14 Beechcraft light patrol craft and jet fuel worth $111 million.[54]

In addition, the Oslo peace accords during the period 1993 to 2000 have physically changed the terrain on which the battle is being fought. The fragmentation of Palestinian territories, as set out in the negotiations, has enabled Israel to exercise much greater control over the West Bank and the Gaza Strip than was possible in 1987. By dividing the Palestinian areas into separate enclaves, cut off from each other by metalled Israeli highways, which are patrolled by Israeli troops, the business of occupation has become more, not less effective:

> *The matrix of control, though it lends a benign and civil face to the occupation, is sustained only by raw military power. The 16 June edition of **Yediot Akhronot** quoted the Israeli Chief of Staff, Shaul Mofaz, speaking before soldiers at the Erez checkpoint in Gaza. 'If tanks are needed,' he declared, 'tanks will be brought in, and if attack helicopters are necessary, attack helicopters will be brought in... Our ability today to cope with confrontations with Palestinians is better than in the past and the events of Nakba Day* [protests to mark the anniversary of the Israeli declaration of independence in 1948] *proved that'.*[55]

There are now at least 100,000 more heavily armed settlers in the Occupied Territories than there were in 1993, representing, in effect, an extra arm of the Israeli military, which has been used increasingly to harry and kill Palestinian fighters and civilians.[56] During the Oslo period Israeli border closures shattered the Palestinian economy.[57] Signs of growth during the first half of 2000 have long been buried by the economic cost of the new uprising.[58]

Ironically, the one aspect of the new intifada which has the most potential to threaten Israeli security is closed off to the current Palestinian leadership. The new militancy of the 'Israeli Arabs' is a serious challenge in the heart of Israel itself. These are the Palestinians living inside Israel's pre-1967 borders. For the first time since the 1970s they rose in revolt as the Occupied Territories went up in flames in

October 2000. The protests in Nazareth and other Palestinian towns were not simply gestures of solidarity—they reflected years of pent-up anger at the systematic racism of the Israeli state. Palestinian villages are prevented from accessing government funds to improve water, electricity or sewage facilities. Palestinians are even prevented from legally building new homes. In the workplace Arab wages are only about one third of the level of Israeli Jews'.[59] In October 2000 the Israeli army shot dead 13 Arab protestors and ignited a protest movement which shook Israeli political opinion to the core.[60] The Palestinians within Israel have the potential to undermine the tacit policy of separation, which Israeli politicians have been putting into practice in the Occupied Territories. Their presence in the heart of Israel—at 20 percent of the Israeli population they form a substantial minority—undermines the entire notion of the Zionist state. Yet the logic of a generation of peace negotiations has pushed the Palestinian leadership towards accepting Israel's right to the land behind the ceasefire lines of 1948, and thus to keep the Palestinians of Israel itself and the Palestinians of the Occupied Territories divided.[61]

These contradictions have been reflected at the level of the Palestinian street organisations. The first intifada represented the coming of age of a generation of militants within the Occupied Territories, who came to form an alternative political centre of gravity to the exiled leadership of the PLO and Fatah in Tunisia.[62] This time the uprising is taking place in the context of an existing Palestinian Authority. The intifada has sharpened the contradictions within organisations such as Fatah, which still retain immense moral authority and organisational weight on the Palestinian streets. One of the effects of the Oslo peace accords was to create a Palestinian police force, which recruited a large number of the militants who had come to political maturity during the first intifada. These men found themselves expected during the years of 'peace' to police and suppress protests against the Israeli occupation in co-operation with Israeli forces. As the confrontations with the Islamist movement Hamas grew sharper, and as the Palestinian Authority became increasingly more corrupt and repressive, the tanzim, Fatah's local activist base, started to challenge the existing PLO leadership to reform. As Graham Usher explains, 'On the one hand, the tanzim provide the military and political base of the PA's rule. On the other, they are its loyal—and yet potentially most seditious—opposition'.[63]

The new intifada has allowed Fatah to rebuild the tanzim, and has cemented the informal alliance between the secular nationalist movement and the Islamists. However, there is a fierce debate within the movement as whole about the direction of the intifada. Fatah's discussion bulletin of July 2001 carried an article addressing this question directly. The author argued in favour of widening the 'popular' aspects of the intifada—the strikes and protests led by local committees—but also for 'the formulation of a clear military and security strategy...in order to shake the confidence of the occupying Zionist forces, to the point where their losses mean they can no longer sustain the occupation'.[64] The accelerating pace of assassinations and the re-emergence of the PFLP as a guerrilla force show that versions of this strategy are being put into practice by a number of the key nationalist organisations.

The problem is that the militarisation of the intifada on its own cannot possibly liberate the Palestinians. The last intifada, which was fought out on far less difficult terrain, resulted in the Oslo peace accords, now rejected by a large proportion of the Palestinians. In any case, the liberation of Palestine is not simply dependent on the conditions within Palestine itself. The role of the Arab states in supporting the US and Israel makes this clear. The impotence of these regimes, themselves the products of the radical anti-colonial movements of the 1950s and 1960s, is a testimony to the impossibility of achieving liberation within the confines of the national state.

The failure of political Islam

The collapse of the dreams of national liberation is a significant factor in the rise of the Islamist movements across the Middle East over the last 20 years. Islamists thread together the struggle in Palestine, the crisis in Iraq, the question of Kashmir, and of course the struggle of the Mujahadeen in Afghanistan into a kind of 'Islamic internationalism' based on the idea of armed confrontation with the forces of imperialism. In many countries, Islamist groups form the main opposition to the compromised local rulers who are the US's local agents. Even before the attacks on the World Trade Centre the Western media portrayed Islamist organisations as one reactionary bloc. In reality, there is little common ground in organisational methods or even on major political questions between many of the Islamist groups, and history has shown time and again that they will not automatically benefit from a crisis in the local regimes.

Islamist groups currently active in the Middle East fall into two broad categories. The first are relatively broad based reformist parties or student groups which operate within the legal or semi-legal framework of the electoral system and the student unions. The second group are highly unstable armed movements, usually small in numbers, which have proved extremely vulnerable to state repression. Only in certain specific cases, in particular in Lebanon and Palestine, have any of the Islamist groups managed to sustain mass movements which have a significant armed cadre. There is a continuous dynamic between the two wings of the Islamist movement. In response to state repression of open, legal activities, small layers of disillusioned activists break with the main movement and turn to illegal paramilitary activities. It is widely accepted that one of the factors which gave the final impetus to Islamic Jihad's decision to assassinate Anwar al-Sadat in 1981 was Sadat's mass arrests of a huge layer of opposition figures from the semi-legal *Gama'at Islamiyya* student movement, including the brother of Khalid al-Islambouli, one of Jihad's key activists.[65] Yet the armed groups have never managed to capture the state on their own and have generally paid the price for confronting the armed might of the ruling class.[66] Neither Jihad nor the Muslim Brotherhood nor the *Gama'at Islamiyya* was able to take advantage of the assassination of Sadat to seize power in Egypt.

The relationship between the Islamist movements and the state has always been contradictory. On one hand the Islamists attract support on the basis of their critique of the existing state. In many countries in the Middle East they appear to be the only credible and consistent opposition force around. Yet these same states have often played a significant role in nuturing Islamist opposition groups in the past as a counterweight to the left.[67] More importantly, the closer mass Islamist movements get to challenging the state, the more their leadership tends to vacillate and attempt to strike a deal with the existing ruling class. Usually this deal is based on the Islamist leaders' ability to control the mass movement they have unleashed, and on a number of occasions this strategy has threatened to completely fracture the movement.[68]

The contradictions within the Palestinian movement Hamas are an example of this process. During the years of the Oslo agreements Hamas fighters appeared to be the only Palestinian militants prepared to confront the forces of occupation. Hamas grew, in the space of less than a decade, into the major opposition to the PLO in the Occupied Territories. The more successful Hamas was in its military operations, the more severe was the Israeli response. This increased the pressure on Yasser Arafat both from the Palestinian street, where Hamas had begun to build a real base in the vacuum left by Fatah, and from Israel which was demanding a clampdown on Hamas activists. On several occasions the leadership of Hamas called off all military operations to relieve the pressure on Arafat, only to find that they could not abruptly 'turn off' the movement they had created, particularly when Israel was increasing the pressure on the Palestinian territories. The tensions within Hamas threatened many times to break into outright warfare, with the younger layer of activists and fighters threatening to ignore the ceasefire declared by the leadership, and even to target some of those same leaders if they continued to co-operate with the Palestinian security forces.[69] This dynamic could be seen at work again in the aftermath of the launch of US air strikes against Afghanistan. Huge student demonstrations in the West Bank were fired upon by the Palestinian police, who killed a number of demonstrators for the first time since the beginning of the new intifada. In response to the police attacks, the Hamas leadership scrambled to strike a deal with Arafat to keep the streets quiet.[70]

If Hamas, despite its mass base, finds it difficult to turn its radical rhetoric into a serious challenge to the Palestinian bourgeoisie, by far the weakest of the local ruling classes, the task facing the armed Islamist cells of al-Qaida is even greater. These disparate groups of armed militants, despite military successes against US targets, have no real connection to the struggles of ordinary people, and no effective way of creating one. As Olivier Roy explained in *Le Monde Diplomatique* in 1998:

> *The social content of the Islamic revolution is foreign to them. In Egypt, for example, the **Gama'at Islamiyya** approved the agrarian counter-reform carried out by Mubarak...they are largely disconnected from the real strategic issues of the Muslim world (except in Pakistan and Afghanistan). Their distinctive feature is their internationalism and their lack of territorial base.[71]*

As armed resistance movements throughout history have discovered time and time again, assassinations and suicide bombings on their own will never shift the balance of social forces in favour of the oppressed. The Islamist movements of the Middle East face the same problems as Fatah and the secular national liberation movements when they opt for a strategy of military confrontation with imperialism. In addition they have offered no alternative for the millions of people across the region whose lives are being wrecked by global capitalism. In many cases the armed groups simply ignore these questions. Where Islamists have had some success gaining access to the structures of the state, for instance in Iran, Sudan, and at the level of local government in Algeria and Turkey, they have often ended up imposing the same economic programmes that they opposed in the past.[72]

Towards an Arab intifada

The only real force for change in the Middle East is the working class. Unlike the liberation movements which have attempted to confront imperialism through the nation state, organised workers clearly have the potential to challenge the existing imperialist order across national borders. In an era when corporations and states organise at an international level to guarantee their profits, an international response from the workers who are paying for the crisis is not only possible but necessary. This is true in the Middle East, just as it is anywhere else in the world. As the events of the last few years show, the impact of neo-liberal policies is rapidly creating the conditions for a social explosion in one or more countries in the Middle East. Structural adjustment and privatisation have provoked strikes and protests across the region. These very processes are not only pushing workers to resist, but also creating a bigger working class, as the case of Saudi Arabia clearly shows. At the same time, the social impact of these policies undermines the ideological basis for neo-liberalism. Opposition activists in Syria are arguing for political liberalisation as a counterpart to economic liberalisation. The experience of Egypt shows clearly that in times of economic crisis structural adjustment can only proceed within a framework of brutal political repression.[73] Although it is only at an early stage, there are some signs that activists in the Middle East are looking closely to the anti-capitalist movement for inspiration. For instance, in response to the planned World Trade Organisation meeting in Qatar in November 2001, Lebanese activist groups organised a counter-conference modelled on the forums of Prague and Genoa to debate the issues of globalisation and imperialism.

Imperialism intensifies the impact of economic crisis across the Middle East by creating conditions in which anger over economic issues can quickly spill over into a more generalised challenge to the system as a whole. The issue of Palestine is a key marker for this process of radicalisation. Demonstrations by students in Egypt at the outbreak of the uprising were quickly joined by workers. Slogans on the protests moved on from demands for the expulsion of the Israeli ambassador to the issues of price rises, government corruption and state repression. Journalists and lawyers also took part in solidarity action including strikes and occupations. Banners and chants attacked the Mubarak regime for its links to Israel and America, and a group of students, following the example of anti-capitalist protests in Prague a few days earlier, smashed up a Kentucky Fried Chicken restaurant.[74]

The war in Afghanistan has only increased the pressure on the local regimes, and on the US. Yet ultimately what will determine whether the anger on the streets develops into a sustained mass movement is a subjective factor—the clarity of its political leadership. The fate of the national liberation movements and the contradictions of the Islamist organisations show that neither of these forces can provide that kind of leadership. The importance of a Marxist analysis of the crisis in the Middle East has never been clearer. The need for revolutionary socialist organisation in the region has never been more urgent.

Notes

Thanks to Dave Renton for comments on the draft of this article, and to Simon Assaf for some of the material on Saudi Arabia.

1 Israeli TV, Jerusalem Channel 2, 7 October 2001.

2 English and Israeli sources usually refer to this area as 'Temple Mount'. The Arabic name for the area is Haram al-sharif, and the mosque is known as the Al-Aqsa Mosque, or the Dome of the Rock (Qubbat al-Sakhara in Arabic).

3 J Burke, 'Bin Laden's Network: Hijacking Suspect Was Bin Laden Bodyguard', *The Observer*, 30 September 2001.

4 R Khalaf, 'Riyadh Fears Fallout From War: Saudi Arabia's Support For The US is Likely to Increase Domestic Unrest', *Financial Times*, 8 October 2001.

5 Ahmad al-Zawahiri appeared beside Osama Bin Laden in the videotaped statement aired by the Qatari satellite broadcaster Al-Jazeera on the night US air-strikes began against Afghanistan. Al-Jazeera, 7 October 2001.

6 V Lenin, *Imperialism: The Highest Stage of Capitalism* (Beijing, 1966). A number of important articles discussing imperialism since the Second World War were published in this journal during the Gulf War. See, for instance, J Rees, 'The New Imperialism', *International Socialism* 48 (Autumn 1990); and A Callinicos, 'Marxism and imperialism', *International Socialism* 50 (Spring 1991).

7 See P Marshall, *Intifada: Zionism, Imperialism and Palestinian Resistance* (London, 1989), for a full discussion of the role played by Zionism and Israel in the Middle East.

8 Egyptian state news agency, MENA, 14 March 2001.

9 R Khalaf, 'Saudi Job Famine That Feeds Terror', *Financial Times*, 19 October 2001.

10 Al-Jazeera, 13 October 2000.

11 Agence France Presse, 'Students Protest Again In Oman Over US Strikes On Afghanistan', 9 October 2001.

12 S Goldenberg, 'Far Right Leader Who Fell Victim To His Own Ideas', *The Guardian*, 18 October 2001.

13 See D Leigh and J Wilson, 'Counting Iraq's Victims', *The Guardian*, 10 October 2001, for a rather sceptical commentary on the origins of these figures.

14 K Sengupta, 'Inside The Pariah's Den: A Special Report On Life In Baghdad Ten Years After The Gulf War', *The Independent*, 24 November 2000.

15 A video of this interview was played at the trial of the men convicted of the 1998 bombings of American embassies in Africa. See CNN, 'Bombers' Defence Focuses On US Policy On Iraq', 4 June 2001, http://www6.cnn.com/2001/LAW /06/04/embassy.bombings.02/

16 P Bennis, 'And They Called It Peace', *Middle East Report* 215 (Summer 2000), www.merip.org

17 UN press release, 17 December 1999, available online at www.fas.org/news/iraq /1999/12/19991217-sc6775.htm

18 R Saad, 'It's Called Genocide', *Al-Ahram Weekly*, 6-12 July 2000, www.ahram. org.eg/weekly/2000/489/focus.htm

19 P Bennis, op cit.

20 D Abdallah, 'Bomb Kills 23 Americans, Wounds 250 In Saudi Arabia', Reuters, 26 June 1996.

21 'The Fatwa Against the Royal Family', *The Economist*, 13 October 2001, p65.

22 Ibid.

23 Quoted in D Hiro, 'America's Shifting Middle East Policy', *Middle East International*, 28 September 2001, p28.

24 Ibid, p29.

25   Energy Information Administration website, http://www.eia.doe.gov/emeu/cabs/saudi.html

26   A Sampson, *The Seven Sisters* (London, 1981), p112.

27   P Marshall, op cit, p75.

28   N MacFarquhar, 'Leisure Class To Working Class In Saudi Arabia', *New York Times*, 26 August 2001.

29   International Confederation of Free Trade Unions, *Annual Survey of Violations of Trade Union Rights* (2001), www.icftu.org

30   C D Masters, E D Attanasi and D H Root, 'World Petroleum Assessment And Analysis', paper given at the Fourteenth World Petroleum Conference, Norway, 1994, and published on the web by United States Geological Survey Eastern Energy Resources Team, http://energy.er.usgs.gov/products/papers /WPC/14/text.htm

31   'Managing A Fluid Situation: Crude Oil Prices Have Fallen More Steeply Than The Market Expected', *Financial Times*, 8 December 2000.

32   *Ukaz* (Jedda), 4 August 2001.

33   N MacFarquhar, op cit.

34   'Gulf States Risk Pointers', *Jane's Sentinel*, 9 May 2001.

35   N MacFarquhar, op cit.

36   G Dinmore, 'Iran Treads Softly Towards Moderation', *Financial Times*, 11 June 2001.

37   Islamic Republic News Agency, 'Consumer Goods Price Index Up By 11.8 Percent For July-August', 14 October 2001. Also on privatisation, see G Dinmore, 'Iran's Workers Vent Sell-Off Frustrations', *Financial Times*, 19 June 2001.

38   R al-Turk, 'al-saubat al-kharijiyya tuakid al-haja ila al-infitah wa itlaq quwa al-shaab', *al-Hayat*, 10 August 2001, p8. Riyad al-Turk's use of the word 'infitah' in the title of this article is indicative of a mood on the left in Syria and Lebanon that economic liberalisation should be combined with greater political openness. The term 'infitah' was used by Anwar al-Sadat, successor to Gamal Abd al-Nasser in Egypt, to describe his 'open door policy' of economic liberalisation. In Egypt the word is associated with the sleazy heyday of Sadat's rule, when ordinary people saw prices rise and living standards fall, but a layer of speculators, known as 'al-munfatihun', made fortunes from government contracts. The internal debate in the Syrian ruling class on this issue reflects the fear among sections of the ruling Ba'ath Party that once the process of liberalisation has begun they will be unable to control it from above.

39   A Abu Khalil, 'Lebanon One Year After The Israeli Withdrawal,' *MERIP Press Information Note* 58, 29 May 2001.

40   'Lebanon's Hariri Re-evaluates Economic Reforms', Reuters, 8 March 2001, and R Baroudi, 'Restructuring the Electricity Sector is the Key to Economic Health', *The Daily Star*, Beirut, 11 October 2001, www.dailystar.com.lb

41   A Morrow, 'Lebanon Shoots Its Wounded', *Business Monthly* (Cairo), August 2001, www.amcham.org.eg/HTML/News_Publication/BusinessMonthly/Aug01

42   *Al-Ahram*, 18 January 1977.

43   H El-Laithy, 'Structural Adjustment and Poverty', in A El-Mahdi (ed), *Aspects of Structural Adjustment in Africa and Egypt*, Center for the Study of Developing Countries (Cairo, 1997), p140.

44   N C Pratt, 'The Legacy Of The Corporatist State: Explaining Workers' Responses To Economic Liberalisation in Egypt', *Durham Middle East Papers* (November 1998), Centre for Middle Eastern and Islamic Studies (Durham, 1998), p24.

45   A El-Mahdi 'The Economic Reform Programme in Egypt After Four Years of Implementation' in A El-Mahdi (ed), op cit, p28.

46   S Nasr, 'Tenants' Fate', *Al-Ahram Weekly*, 25 February-3 March 1999.

47   D Buchan, 'A Return To Agrarian Capitalism', *Financial Times*, 10 May 2000.

48 T Mitchell, 'Dreamland: The Neoliberalism of Your Desires', *Middle East Report* 210, http://www.merip.org
49 Ibid.
50 S Aburish, 'The Coming Arab Crash', *The Guardian*, 18 October 2001.
51 See, for instance, Ahdaf Soueif on the powerful impact of Al-Jazeera in A Soueif, 'It Provides The One Window Through Which We Can Breathe', *The Guardian*, 9 October 2001.
52 Y Stein, 'Events On The Temple Mount—September 29 2000: Interim Report', B'Tselem, www.btselem.org
53 Health, Development, Information and Policy Institute, 'Factsheet: Palestinian Intifada (28 September 2000-13 September 2001)', www.hdip.org
54 A Barzilay, 'IAF's Largest Ever Helicopter Deal With US Seen Ending Crisis Over Phalcon Affair', *Ha'aretz*, 3 October 2000.
55 J Halper, 'The 94 Percent Solution: A Matrix Of Control', *Middle East Report* 216, www.merip.org
56 See, for instance, Amnesty International report on the sentence given to Nahum Korman, an Israeli citizen who killed a Palestinian girl of 11. He was ordered to complete six months community service, while Su'ad Hilmi Ghazal, a 15 year old Palestinian girl who injured an Israeli settler, was jailed for six and a half years. Amnesty International, 'Israel/Occupied Territories: Impunity for Killers of Palestinians', 24 January 2001 (MDE/004/2001), www.amnesty.org
57 A Alexander, 'Powerless in Gaza: The Palestinian Authority and the Myth of the Peace Process', *International Socialism* 89 (Winter 2000), pp41-43.
58 S Roy, 'The Palestinian Economy After Oslo: Decline and Disfigurement', in R Carey (ed), *The New Intifada* (London, 2001).
59 See reports by the Arab Association for Human Rights at www.arabhra.org
60 Palestinians within Israel are frequently attacked by the right for their lack of 'loyalty' to Israel. In August this year the education minister, Limor Livnat, proposed that Arab schools which commemorated Nakba Day to mark the loss of Palestine in 1948, instead of Israeli independence, should be barred from accessing extra funding unless they could prove their loyalty to the Israeli state. A Fisher-Ilan, 'Ben-Shabbat Rips Livnat's Linking Loyalty To School Funding', *Jerusalem Post*, 27 August 2001, www.jpost.com/Editions/2001/08/27/News/News.33457.html
61 See M Sid-Ahmed, 'The Israeli Arabs', *Al-Ahram Weekly*, 14-20 December 2000, for an analysis of the contradictions involved from an Egyptian perspective.
62 See G Andoni, 'A Comparative Study of Intifada 1987 and Intifada 2000', in R Carey, op cit, for a full discussion of the contrasts between the two intifadas.
63 G Usher, 'Fatah's Tanzim: Origins And Politics', *Middle East Report* 217, www.merip.org
64 'Intifada: Miwazin al-Quwa', *Fatah*, issue 13, vol 37 (first half of July 2001), p25.
65 G Kepel, *The Prophet And Pharoah* (London, 1985), p210.
66 See C Harman, 'The Prophet And The Proletariat', *International Socialism* 64 (Autumn 1994), pp3-63 for a comprehensive analysis of the Islamist movement.
67 G Kepel, op cit, pp138-141.
68 See C Harman, op cit, pp30-37.
69 M al-Dirassat al-Ishtirakiyya, *Filastin: Ruyia Thawriyya* (Cairo, 2001).
70 Ismail Abu Shanab, Hamas spokesman at the Islamic University, told reporters after the police shot a 13 year old boy dead, 'These events are regrettable. We live under aggressive occupation and we must turn all our efforts to resisting the occupation'—H Morris, 'Palestinian Police Shoot Dead Two Protesters', *Financial Times*, 9 October 2001.

71   O Roy, 'Fundamentalists Without A Common Cause', *Le Monde Diplomatique*, October 1998, www.en.monde-diplomatique.fr/1998/10/04afghan. See also Roy's book, *The Failure of Political Islam* (Cambridge, Mass, 1994).

72   C Harman, op cit, pp49-54.

73   See, for instance, numerous Amnesty statements available at www.amnesty.org , including 'Egypt Fails To End Torture', 7 May 1998 (MDE 12/23/98), 'Prison Conditions And Deaths In Custody', 24 September 1998 (MDE 12/46/98), 'Hafez Abu Sa'ada Returns To Egypt: Authorities Must Stop Now Harassment Of Human Rights Defenders', 10 March 2000 (MDE 12/08/00).

74   M al-Dirassat al-Ishtirakiyya, op cit.

The poisoned embrace: Plan Colombia and the expansion of imperial power

MIKE GONZALEZ

Colombia (so often misspelt and so rarely understood) has hit the headlines in Britain just twice in 2001—once when a British oil company employee was kidnapped by the ELN (Colombia's National Liberation Army), and again when three alleged members of the IRA were arrested as they left the territories under the control of the FARC (Revolutionary Armed Forces of Colombia, the country's largest guerrilla organisation). Despite the many column inches devoted to these incidents for the day or two that media interest lasted, little was done to dispel the stereotypical image of a Latin America populated almost entirely by guerrillas, drug dealers and generals in dark glasses. Certainly there was no attempt to take the opportunity to explain why the US government has thus far given over $1 billion in aid under the auspices of Plan Colombia, nor why the vast bulk of that money has been spent on military training and weapons, despite the repeated assertions from US State Department sources that the central purpose of the aid programme is to eliminate drug production.[1] Mo Mowlam was one politician recruited for the campaign to reassure the world of the high moral purposes of Plan Colombia. She briefly graced the front pages of the British press kneeling beside a dead coca plant—living proof that the Blair government's support for Plan Colombia was one more component of its ethical foreign policy.

The reality, of course, is far more sinister and more far reaching. Equally clear is the fact that even a successful outcome of Plan Colombia will have virtually no effect on the rising graph of drug use in the US. Whether the British government is just deeply disingenuous, or a willing accomplice in the concealment of the realities of a new period of expansion and militarisation whose horizons lie far beyond Colombia, is unproven.[2] The evidence, however, is accumulating relentlessly, as human rights groups, NGOs, guerrilla organisations, striking trade unionists and social movements give notice to the world of what is happening to Colombia, and as hundreds of thousands of displaced people and refugees fleeing from areas of conflict and destruction offer poignant witness to the real objectives of Plan Colombia.

The genesis of Plan Colombia

Plan Colombia was presented to the Colombian Congress by its current president, Andres Pastrana, in 1999. It was strongly rumoured that the Spanish version he offered them was a translation of a version originally written in English and discussed during a visit to President Clinton in Washington. Whatever the truth, there is no doubt that 'Plan Colombia is both a continuation and an escalation of US politico-military policy...adapted to new global realities'.[3] That was not how it was represented. Pastrana's justification for the plan was that it offered a strategy for restoring stability and peace to Colombia, a country whose modern history has been characterised by violence and conflict. The centrepiece of the policy, ostensibly at least, was a drugs eradication programme. The relationship between the two was that Clinton would thus be able to argue at home that the plan was not a military intervention in Latin America but rather an extension of domestic drugs containment policies. Pastrana for his part could argue that the plan identified the drug producers as the central obstacle to democracy in the country. The $1 billion of aid that Clinton sought from Congress was overwhelmingly devoted to arms and military spending. The only other measure was a large-scale programme of defoliant spraying intended, it was alleged, to eliminate coca and poppy production while leaving other crops unscathed.

It certainly seems that the British government, among others, has bought the drugs eradication story—accepting without demur the suggestion that the large guerrilla organisations and their continuing confrontation with the Colombian state were no more than extensions of the drug war. A new term—'narcoguerrillas'—was coined to make the elision easier. Thus the US State Department was able to report on 30 June 2001 that 'the US Congress gave final passage June 30 to an $11,200 million spending bill that includes $1,300 million in emergency aid designed to *help the government of Colombia battle the illegal drug trade*'.[4]

It became immediately clear, however, that the US government was fully aware that the likely effect on drug trafficking into America's cities would be negligible—previous eradication programmes had demonstrated that beyond question. Public statements from the Colombian government seemed entirely concerned with defeating the guerrillas, while the spokespersons for the US government were clearly preoccupied with matters of 'regional security'.

The net effect of this eradication programme has been the increasing militarisation of Colombian society, the displacement of up to 2 million people, and the creation of a deepening economic crisis whose victims include the small farmers, oil and transport workers, and urban refugees who have repeatedly demonstrated their concerns in the streets of Colombia's cities in recent months.

The claim of the plan's US sponsors to be concerned with the restoration of human rights and the consolidation of democracy was a veil that covered completely different purposes. The direct consequence of that aid package has been to legitimise a whole range of assaults on all democratic rights, to militarise all aspects of civil society and to subordinate the interests of the majority of Colombians to the geopolitical concerns of global capitalism.

Drugs—myth and reality

The Colombian drugs boom began in the 1960s when the northern regions around Santa Marta provided marijuana, much prized in the booming US market. The result was a kind of gold rush along Colombia's Caribbean coast, when the infamous Cherokee Chieftains with smoked glass windows signalled the arrival of a newly rich class. When US authorities began to control that trade, the weed was replaced by cocaine which was much more profitable and less bulky.[5] The raw material was the coca plant, grown by peasants and small farmers in Bolivia and Peru, then collected in unmarked planes and taken to small laboratories and processing plants in the Amazon regions before export to the US and, in smaller quantities, to Europe. The profits were unimaginable, even when they had to be shared with the ruling elites of a number of Latin American countries. In Bolivia, for example, the military regimes of the 1970s were deeply involved in this continental drug trade.[6] The involvement of US-based agencies, and the CIA in particular, is murkier, though arms for drugs exchanges were to emerge into the public arena in the following decade, with the testimonies of Oliver North and others.

Colombia's geography lent itself well to the creation of hidden jungle laboratories and the trade routes had already been laid out during the marijuana years. Now Medellín became the centre of this new drug trade—dominated first by Carlos Lehder and later by Pablo Escobar.[7] This group had emerged from the poorer urban sectors, and they ensured their loyalty by generous acts of charity. But the scale of profits involved in the trade gave the drug cartels the ability to buy and sell politicians, lawyers, judges and generals—and to murder those who refused to comply. In 1990 the Medellín cartel murdered three presidential candidates. Escobar was boasting that he could pay off the national debt, or take on the Colombian army and win. As was to be expected, the Colombian ruling classes found this challenge intolerable. While it was always true that Colombian society was deeply divided and cross-hatched by regional power bases,[8] and that the state was a point of negotiation between them, in the final analysis Escobar was challenging the power of the ruling classes as a whole. And even if, as subsequent years would demonstrate, those classes had been corrupted and controlled by the drug cartels, they could not tolerate an alternative power within the nation state. The grandfather of the cartel, Lehrer, was now in prison in the US. Washington was demanding the extradition of the current cartel leaders too. Escobar therefore reached an agreement with the government to turn himself in, in exchange for a guarantee that he would not be extradited. A special jail was built for him—but it quickly became clear that it was effectively a fortified hotel with state protection, since he quite openly continued to conduct his business from there. In any event, he walked out in 1992 and remained in hiding until his assassination at the hands of Colombian anti-drugs agencies a year later. Power then moved to the competing Cali cartel, which explicitly spurned any aspirations to power. In 1995 its leader, Rodriguez Orijuela, was also arrested, just as the extent of its involvement in and control of the government of Ernesto Samper—the very government that had proclaimed its resolve to crush the cartels—began to emerge with mounting supporting evidence.

The effect of this and other anti-drug measures promoted by the US government was negligible. In the 1980s major interventions in Bolivia and Peru—the chief source of the coca leaf—had simply resulted in a shift in the areas of primary production towards southern Colombia. The traffic found different routes and expanded onto a worldwide terrain that embraced Turkey, Albania, Central America and Mexico as the chief portals to the European and US markets respectively. The long and short of it was that the spectacular assaults on coca and poppy growing areas only affected the smallest cog in the system—the peasant growers. Since the coca plant gives a crop in 60 days, it took very little time for new crops to be grown elsewhere:

According to a 1999 General Accounting Office (GAO) report, 'Despite two years of extensive herbicide spraying [in Colombia], *US estimates show* [that] *net coca cultivation actually increased by 50 percent'.[9]*

In fact:

Even if 'successful' eradication were actually achieved in Colombia, there are 1.6 billion acres in the rest of the biophysically hospitable Amazon. That is more than 2,000 times the 740,000 acres needed to fulfil the complete international demand for cocaine. **In the entire history of the use of force against illicit crops, not one effort has succeeded in reducing the supply of natural drugs needed to fully supply the world market.[10]**

The reality, then, is that the fundamental issue is the demand, not the supply—and the US government, while willing to disburse tens of millions in spectacular interventions in the affairs of supplier countries, refuses to address the issue of why drugs are used to the extent that they are in the US. While there seems in recent times to have been a slight decline in middle class use of drugs as their harmful effects have been documented and publicised, the inner city poor have no alternative. They are criminalised and the small-scale dealers are added to the millions in America's prisons. Meanwhile, an estimated 50 percent of the half a trillion dollars of profit that drugs yield every year remains within the financial system of the US itself, reinvested and manipulated by some 500 or so economic actors.[11]

Within Colombia itself the Medellín and Cali cartels have been successfully broken, but this has not meant even a momentary break in the flow of drugs. Local production is now in the hands of several hundred middle size refiners and distributors whose task it is to pass it on to the major actors in the traffic.

The US, meanwhile, continues with its policy of spraying crops across southern Colombia. There has been a sinister change, however, under the aegis of Plan Colombia, the effects of which are likely to be profound and destructive in both social and economic terms. For nearly two decades the use of the herbicide glyphosate, it is claimed, has eliminated some 150,000 acres of land devoted to the cultivation of coca and poppy plants. Yet, as we have seen, the effects on overall production were relatively small. In recent times the fields have been sprayed with a different agent—the myoherbicide *Fusarium oxysporum*—whose effects are far reaching and indiscriminate. It kills a wide range of plants, and will almost certainly have catastrophic effects on the fragile ecology of the region.[12] Even more curious, and a point to which I shall return, is that, while 40 percent of Colombia's coca is currently grown in the *north* of the country, spraying is concentrated in the *south*.

This issue is complex and its ramifications need to be considered in more detail elsewhere. But at another level, the irresistible conclusion is quite a simple one. The drug eradication programme which ostensibly lies at the heart of Plan Colombia is incapable of realising its own goals—as all previous drug eradication programmes pursued in the last two decades have repeatedly demonstrated. This is well known in State Department circles and reiterated in every debate on the issue. We must therefore assume that the 'war on drugs' is the veil behind which hides a very different strategy.

Strategies in the backyard

Plan Colombia, as Petras emphasises, is the latest chapter in a long narrative of counter-insurgency—the succession of policies and strategies whereby the US protects the economic interests of its home-based capital.[13] Thus the military intervention in Cuba, Puerto Rico and Nicaragua at the turn of the century both provided a bridgehead to guard its 'backyard' and ensured a security fence to protect the activities of the United Fruit Company among others. Its surrogates and representatives were on hand to crush Chile's 100-day republic in 1930, the 1932 insurrection in El Salvador, the 1933 rising in Cuba and so on.

The Cuban Revolution of 1959 ushered in a new period of counter-insurgency, which combined military, economic and ideological interventions under the twin banners of the Alliance for Progress and the Inter American Security Treaty. The objective was to isolate Cuba, provide alternative routes to reform within the imperial context and impede any growth in the development of guerrilla warfare across the continent. The iron fist emerged from the velvet glove of reform in September 1973, when Chile's experiment in radical transformation through parliament was destroyed by a US-supported military coup led, among others, by Augusto Pinochet, who eventually emerged as its undisputed head. The Chilean coup was not just a local matter, but a strategy of militarisation and enforced economic integration. The 'Chilean miracle', proclaimed by Thatcher and others, effectively subjected workers to the laws of the market in their most brutal form while destroying their organisations of self defence. It is ironic to hear the mock horror expressed by Western leaders when the co-ordination of repression by the military regimes of the southern cone (Plan Condor) emerged into full public view during the Pinochet trial. That regionalisation of the conflict and the co-ordination of strategies between the new military governments was the hallmark of US thinking throughout this period.

The Nicaraguan Revolution of 1979 turned the arrow around—suddenly it was pointing at the heart of the beast. The Central American region was in turmoil, and a mass movement in El Salvador made the possibility of a regional revolutionary process a real one. In the event, the Sandinista government of Nicaragua chose to disengage the fate of its revolution from the intensifying struggle in the rest of the region.[14] It did not save it, of course, from systematic assault—military, economic and ideological—from the north, the destruction of its economy, the death of some 60,000 of its citizens and the wounding of twice that number. It is one of the many tragic ironies of Latin America's recent past that the consequence of US policy in the region through the 1980s was to systematically destroy the Sandinista attempt to develop an independent social economy and return both Nicaragua and its neighbours to a servile dependence on the very drug trade the US now denounces.

US strategy in Central America in the 1980s was characterised by 'low intensity operations'—a misnomer if ever there was one:

Through the application of a flexible mix of aid blockades, trade sanctions, economic sabotage, political and psychological pressures, civic action 'pacification' programs, military warfare and electoral intervention, Reagan-Bush policy has attempted to consolidate or install in power in Central America elected governments willing to accommodate White House objectives—not least in the economic sphere.[15]

Petras's definition hardly captures the human costs of the policy—the tens of thousands dead, the destruction of economies, the displacement of millions towards the slums around the capital cities, the creation of monstrous corps of murderers like the Nicaraguan Contras with their specialities in the dismemberment of living bodies, the creation of a kind of counter-reform in the countryside where large swathes of land are restored to the landowners, often through the actions of peasant militias. The militarisation of society, the implantation of terror in the countryside, renders any and all forms of self-organisation or self-defence impossible. The role of the US lay in supporting internal counter-revolutionary forces, reinforcing the military through direct military aid and the provision of trainers, using international financial and other agencies to isolate and undermine the local economy, and mobilising a massive propaganda apparatus across the world.

After nearly a decade of struggle and resistance the peace accords of 1989 in El Salvador and the fall of the Sandinista government in 1990[16] were to usher in a new era. We now know what that new era looks like. In southern Honduras, which had provided the base for anti-Sandinista operations through the 1980s, the economy was destroyed and the population corrupted and prostituted by the Contras and their US advisers.

Agricultural production in the whole frontier region virtually ceased as the population fled the Contra war. Drugs regularly supplied to US military personnel and their allies turned the area into a boom zone for some and an important transition route for the drug trade. In El Salvador the economy is now wholly reintegrated into the world market, most food is imported and unemployment is endemic. Nicaragua's economy collapsed through the period of the Contra war, but unsurprisingly the promised post-election aid never arrived. Now Nicaragua too has all the familiar characteristics of an impoverished economy open to the ravages of a world system—unemployment rates hovering around 60 percent, a horrific drug problem, a collapsing infrastructure, an agricultural sector where living standards are unimaginably low, and a tiny middle class living comfortable lives under siege conditions. In every case the leaders of the guerrilla organisations of the 1980s led the peace negotiations and were absorbed into the new governments. In El Salvador and Nicaragua many of the ex-guerrillas entered the army and the police. They then found themselves to be functionaries of the neo-liberal or 'structural adjustment' policies whose net effect was to subject those in whose name they had so recently been fighting to the laws of a confident and barbaric world market.[17] Most brutally paradoxical of all, perhaps, was that the ex-guerrillas found themselves co-operating with those who had been guilty of the most appalling human rights atrocities and in many cases negotiating their impunity as a condition of the 'peace' process. It is particularly poignant to travel through Nicaragua today, and see the living conditions of those who fought the Contra war compared with the luxurious lifestyle and ostentatious wealth of many of those who led that war.

That, then, is the background to Plan Colombia. The strategic priorities of US policy—the destruction of resistance in order to create an open terrain for international capital, and US-based capital in particular—have been consistently pursued through the countries of the southern cone in the 1970s and Central America in the 1980s. It is those same geopolitical imperatives that impel US policy in Colombia today, though the scale of things has changed. Clinton's legacy to Latin America—Plan Colombia—both continues and develops that policy, adding significant new resources, reinvoking a right to intervention by redefining the issue as a domestic US matter (the campaign against drugs), and emphasising its international and regional nature. To that must be added, however, the reality of a world entering the 21st century in an era of globalisation on the one hand, and mounting resistance to globalisation on the other.

The outlays envisaged by Plan Colombia amount to $1.3 billion. The distribution of that finance is revealing—82 percent of it will go to directly military purposes, divided between helicopters for the anti-drugs battalion of the Colombian army (47 percent), sea and river operations (27 percent) and 7 percent to the national police. Of the remainder just over 11 percent will be dedicated to alternative development projects and 7 percent towards the defence of human rights![18] This leaves very little room for doubt as to the repressive purposes of Plan Colombia. It is a *military* project whose objective is control over the southern regions of Colombia. Furthermore it is not limited to Colombia itself. The six-year projection within the plan assumed the progressive involvement of what are described there as 'partner nations'. The real significance of the term is already emerging, as the Ecuadorean government has been 'persuaded' to cede the Manta air base and its hinterland near the Colombian border to the US.

But even were the distribution of the total package to be altered—were alternative development to be given more, for example—nothing would be changed. For the allocation to human rights and alternative crops is determined within the wider context of the plan—that is within the framework of a geopolitics whose strategic purposes involve the 'rooting out' of coca and poppy production from the area by military and chemical means. As the new more aggressive spraying policy begins to affect other crops, and as the confrontation between the military and the guerrilla forces grows more intense (for what other purpose can the cascade of new military material into the area have?), tens or hundreds of thousands of peasants will join the fleeing columns making for the larger cities. They will not only be escaping the increasingly generalised violence—they will also be moving because their very livelihood has been destroyed. Others, however, will swell the ranks of the guerrillas for identical reasons (I will return to the issue in greater detail in the final sections below) and provide legitimacy for a mounting and costly military campaign. It is already the case that Colombian society is becoming increasingly militarised as a result of Plan Colombia—not only because the armed forces now have enormous logistical and ideological support from the powerful northern neighbour, but also because the priorities of the Colombian government are increasingly military. As the tide of refugees grows and the availability of basic foods declines, so the repression currently focused on the areas under guerrilla domination will generalise and intensify. This is not an imagined outcome—it is already a reality. The public sector and transport strikes of July this year were testimony to the social effects of Plan Colombia.

It is perfectly clear that for some time the Colombian state has been unable to control or contain the strains and contradictions within the society. Shot through with corruption, nepotism and conflicts between regional and sectoral interests, the state has—it seems to me—effectively crumbled into warring factions squabbling over the booty. Each new president—Pastrana, the current incumbent, among them—has set out to impose human rights and developmental priorities, yet in each case revelations of complicity, corruption and the exchange of favours have rendered those promises meaningless. Those public servants, and there have been many, who have attempted to act democratically have been cut down in their hundreds and thousands.

In the latter half of the 1980s it did appear that a political space was opening in parallel with the settlements reached between the leaderships of the armed struggle and the state in Central America. But as elements in the Colombian state opened dialogue with the M-19 and the FARC guerrillas, many within the military establishment were demanding a military solution. Those who came in from the cold to negotiate and became candidates in the elections of 1990 were almost all murdered, while trade union leaders and militants in social movements were assassinated in growing numbers. The assault on the cocaine barons, by contrast, yielded almost nothing. Some were captured and some killed, but the structures of their invisible order remained intact.

The reality was that the Colombian state was powerless to impose any kind of national solution or to initiate a process of reform. While the army complained bitterly that it was perpetually being restrained in its counter-guerrilla activity, and darkly criticised the political agenda and the concept of peace as essentially the concession of victory to the guerrillas, the political class was so compromised and corrupt that it did not and could not seize the window that had briefly opened for it.[19] The army's frustration expressed itself in the growth of the paramilitary organisations that terrorised populations and waged a private and undocumented war against the rural population in particular. It is quite clear that these were the irregulars of the Colombian army, and that in many cases their connections with the military were intimate and immediate.[20] On the other hand, they were also directly connected to the drug cartels—or were instruments of rival factions. This did not stop them enjoying the covert support of sections of the army, the political class, and indeed US agencies like the CIA. It is bitterly ironic that one of the principal leaders of the paramilitary gangs, Carlos Castaño, is now offering himself as a broker between the Colombian government, the drug barons and the US government.[21] For any who imagined that Plan Colombia would bring the paramilitaries under control, or limit their activities, this is the most public of replies. The paramilitaries will now become effectively absorbed into a strategy of military containment and control—and their leaders, like Castaño, will be incorporated into the structures of a new, militarised state. *Colombia Report* (4 June 2001) reported a bill recently passed in the Colombian Senate which, among other things, provided virtual immunity to members of the armed forces who commit human rights abuses while combating 'supposed' terrorist groups. In what may be a sign of things to come, 2,500 members of the Colombian army seized towns in Nariño province as part of the 'anti-drugs' Operation Tsunami—110 people were killed, only 18 of whom were guerrillas.

Friends and enemies

What are the perspectives that inform US policy in Latin America? The framework for Plan Colombia is marked by two key dates as far as economic policy is concerned. In January 1994 the long-prepared North America Free Trade Area (NAFTA) was announced, drawing Canada, Mexico and the US into a tariff-free zone of economic activity, which represented the first stage in a new phase of global economic integration. This was not simply a trade agreement, but the creation of a single economic unit dominated by US capital. After all, transnational capital had already found a comfortable home in a Mexican economy which had undergone massive privatisation of state assets under the Salinas presidency (1988-1994) and whose financial markets had already been thrown open to external involvement. This was definitely an announcement of things to come. The next stage of this aggressive process of continental integration was already envisaged, with the extension of NAFTA into Central America and the subsequent creation of the Free Trade Area of the Americas (FTAA) which was finally agreed, with sirens and the explosion of teargas canisters as background music, at Quebec City in April 2001.

At the same time, the confidence of the principal actors in the institutions of world capitalism was slightly shaken at the very moment of NAFTA's inception by a 'small local difficulty' whose symbolic impact on the world was far greater than its material effect. The Zapatista rising in Chiapas stole the headlines from the spin doctors of the multinational financial institutions and raised a cry—'Ya Basta!'—which would very soon resonate across a growing worldwide anti-capitalist movement.[22] It would seem that the much vaunted 'end of history' was now over (if the paradox may be excused)—resistance was back on the agenda, placed there by sections of the community at the very margins of the global system—yet, as its leader Marcos so eloquently argued, directly suffering the consequences of the structural adjustment of the new neo-liberal economic order.

It was clear that the Andean region had a key role to play in the expansion plans of global capital. Venezuela (now no longer necessarily a 'partner nation') was a key supplier of oil in the region, but Colombia possesses major deposits of oil and natural gas, currently exploited by foreign multinationals and distributed through the state oil enterprise Ecopetrol. The scale of deposits means that Colombia will become a powerful player in the world oil trade. To a lesser extent so too will neighbouring Ecuador. Control of these resources—as well as other important export areas like flowers and other commodities—is crucial to the growth and expansion of the regional 'free trade' area. Ecuador's economy has already been 'dollarised'—that is, integrated into a global economy. Venezuela, on the other hand, is now run by the nationalist-populist Chavez regime. His rhetoric is clearly rooted in a politics of national liberation and anti-imperialism, and he has followed through by establishing friendly and co-operative arrangements with Cuba, including cut-price oil. Furthermore, OPEC's new president is a Venezuelan. Chavez's actual attitude to the US is less easy to measure, and there are hints that he will be prepared to deal with the US. The future of the region, the fulcrum on which a whole geopolitics is balanced, is therefore Colombia: 'Plan Colombia has to be seen as an attempt to behead the most advanced, radicalised and well organised opposition to US hemispheric hegemony'.[23] Petras's rather adulatory characterisation of the guerrilla organisations, and particularly FARC, will need some added nuances. But his overall explanation of Plan Colombia's greater purposes is, I think, undeniable. For Winfred Tate too, the US is 'gearing up to repeat the mistakes of the past'.[24] That may well be its intention, but as the year 2001 has unfolded it has become increasingly clear that there is a growing resistance to the strategies of globalisation, not only in a burgeoning worldwide anti-capitalist current, but also in a growing Latin American resistance. The implementation of FTAA has been met with rolling strikes in Argentina, while in Bolivia the victory of the mass front in Cochabamba against an attempted water privatisation has been an inspiration. And despite the advancing integration of its economy into global structures, Ecuador has borne witness to an inspiring struggle of indigenous peoples and working class organisations which began in 1990 with the formation of CONAIE, the Ecuadorean Indigenous Peoples Confederation.

But the major test of the geopolitical strategies of the US and global capital is undoubtedly Colombia. It occupies a highly strategic location on the continent, bridging the Caribbean and the Pacific, and dominating the northern part of the continent. Its resources are considerable. But the key consideration, in my view, is political. In the era of globalisation the capacity of capital to gain access to all terrain—the absence of any key region outside its control—becomes a central issue. The history of guerrilla warfare in Colombia has been a very particular one. As a result there do exist well defended and well supported guerrilla enclaves where the cost of a military incursion could well be very high. But it is also a test of capital's resolve and its power, and Vietnam weighs heavy on the memory of the US ruling class. There is not, as some commentators have suggested, a direct parallel to be drawn between Colombia and Vietnam. There is no long history of colonial war, no national liberation struggle as such, no international power struggle reflected in the specific arena. The liberated territories under FARC control do not correspond to the existence of a state (North Vietnam) with its own mass military organs. If, on the other hand, the comparison is with the possibility that the US may find itself compelled to commit large numbers of US troops in the face of the collapse of its local surrogate and the decomposition of the military command (as in South Vietnam), then I think this unlikely too. The Colombian army is numerous and well organised, all the more so with the high level of training and support it has received throughout the 1990s (and not just since the implementation of Plan Colombia) from the US. What Plan Colombia does represent is an escalation of that involvement—and a clear perception on the part of the US that the Colombian state was not able to co-ordinate or impose a political solution across the national territory. Pastrana is only the latest in a series of modernising presidential candidates committed, at least verbally, to processes of reform, who have found themselves unable to create the conditions to make that happen. The 'peace process', which brought the guerrilla leaders and the government into dialogue, was destroyed by the paramilitaries with the complicity of both the army command and the drug cartels. Each attempt to renew the process has produced a similar response. The agreement to a demilitarised zone (*zona de despeje*) in late 1998 and the security guarantees given to the guerrilla forces by the Pastrana government produced an ill concealed fury in the army command—and while the zone still exists, Plan Colombia itself is the guarantee that its existence will be brief.

A catastrophic equilibrium?

Plan Colombia clearly represents, at one level, an attempt by the US to break what it sees as a stalemate in Colombia: a weak state overseeing a divided country with a number of power centres; significant guerrilla armies controlling extensive territories embracing numerous largely peasant populations; combative trade union and human rights organisations exposing the actions of the paramilitaries and the deepening economic crisis; the paramilitaries linked to the armed forces at an earlier stage, yet now acting independently both as a repressive force and as an economic actor; and the multiple participants in a drug economy whose major beneficiaries almost certainly operate outside Colombia but who are themselves wealthy and powerful and able to act independently of state and army.

Who, then, will tip the balance? The US clearly sees itself in that role, reinforcing the interests of the Colombian bourgeoisie, imposing the rule of a strong militarised state and successfully defeating the opposition.

But can the guerrillas be defeated? The major guerrilla organisations the FARC (Revolutionary Armed Forces of Colombia), the ELN (National Liberation Army) and the ERP (People's Revolutionary Army) have long but different histories. The FARC, under its legendary leader Manuel Marulanda or Tirofijo, meaning 'sureshot', emerged during the years of *La Violencia*, the 14-year period during which all political life in Colombia was played out in armed conflict. *La Violencia* began with the assassination in the capital, Bogotá, of a trade unionist and Liberal presidential candidate, Jorge Eliécer Gaitán. The violent reaction to his death began in the capital, but set in motion a process in which social struggles 'degenerated into local party feuds'.[25] That is not to say that there were not issues of class at work—the period prior to *La Violencia* had seen major trade union struggles on the one hand and battles over land and peasant rights on the other. But in the appalling atmosphere of violence unleashed in 1948, it was local chieftains who organised guerrillas to carry out revenge attacks or to settle scores against peasants or rural communities that had opposed them in the past. In some areas the Communist Party began to organise armed peasant defence and to introduce the land issue into its demands. But the irony was that this was a boom time for the Colombian bourgeoisie. Industrial production rose while wages fell—small wonder when all forms of independent organisation were repressed in both city and countryside. In the second half of the 1950s successive governments tried to negotiate an end to the violence, yet each amnesty or ceasefire produced more violence and death. In any event, the amnesties did not apply to the Communist Party, which had now grouped several thousand peasant families into areas of the south known as the independent republics, like Marquetalia. In 1963 these were invaded and crushed by the Colombian army. Those who escaped the subsequent repression formed mobile guerrilla groups, which met (for the second time), in 1966 to form the FARC.[26]

The FARC is indelibly marked by the circumstances of its birth. It emerged first as, and has remained in essence, an organisation of peasant self defence. Its association with the Communist Party did not mean that it was ideologically driven. It responded in pragmatic ways to the changing demands of its social base—which might explain its survival and continuity for over 40 years (a record no other armed guerrilla organisation in Latin America can claim). In the anarchic conditions of the Colombian countryside it has in many ways constituted both a form of local administration and, as Jenny Pearce puts it, 'virtually a rural civil guard'. As a result it has survived through crises that have almost destroyed the other guerrilla groupings. As violence, official and paramilitary, has continued to characterise daily life for most of Colombia's rural population, organised self defence has increasingly become the major issue, but the base of FARC is among small farmers living in precarious conditions. Many of them grow coca—and FARC has taken a tax from this, as from all other activities in the areas under its control. This has allowed the US and its allies to coin the term 'narcoguerrillas'—and to lump FARC together with the drug-producing cartels as if they were two faces of the same phenomenon. Their profits seem to be modest—they have very few of the trappings of the servants of the drug cartels, no AK-47s or Russian secondhand submarines. Most of their weapons are still homemade.[27] They also appear to be highly disciplined and to punish any violation with some ruthlessness. Petras avers that 'in most of their dealings with the rural population, the FARC represents order, rectitude and social justice'.[28] He goes on to say that 'the strength of the FARC is based on the interplay of ideological appeals and the resonance of its analysis and political practices with the everyday reality of peasant life'. This sentence seems to me to contain some studied evasions, since their ideology has changed over time. Rooted in a Communist Party tradition, the FARC adopted a more pragmatic and nationalist position through the 1970s and won considerable support in the process. This was reflected in the UP, the *Unión Patriótica* formed in 1984 as an electoral front, and which won a significant number of parliamentary seats in 1986. In anticipation of later developments in Central America, the government's strategy here was to transform the guerrilla organisation into a political party. But in 1985 the seizure of the Palace of Justice by the guerrilla organisation M-19, and the subsequent killing of over 100 people by the army, initiated a period of renewed repression. M-19's positions were curious and sometimes contradictory, but in the late 1970s and early 1980s it won widespread support, particularly among the urban poor. One poll conducted in 1985 suggested that, should it stand for election, M-19 would win 36.7 percent of the vote. But its relationship with the FARC (some of its founders had been expelled from FARC in the early 1970s) remained tense. The systematic murder of most of the leading members of M-19 after the Palace of Justice events effectively eliminated it from the scene. But the repression fell on all the other armed organisations too.

The FARC's rival, the ELN, was founded in the mid-1960s by students, intellectuals and left wing priests, and was based on the Cuban model. It has undergone a series of internal crises and splits, but currently prevails in areas of the north and centre of the country. While FARC entered into a protracted series of negotiations with the government from the mid-1980s, ELN refused to follow it and organised for armed insurgency, seeking to build a common front with some of the mass organisations that were merging in the 1980s. Nevertheless their methods have continued to rest on the perception of the guerrillas as substitutes for the masses. Kidnappings, particularly of oil company employees, have gained them the resources for survival. In 1993 the FARC declared a renewed military offensive in the face of stagnation in the peace negotiations, just at the time when ELN for the first time was opening discussions with the government of Ernesto Samper. Under Pastrana the talks with the ELN have remained in suspension, while he has reopened discussions with the FARC.

Behind the painful and tortuous progress of negotiations, however, Plan Colombia resolutely advances in its preparations for the eventual destruction of the guerrilla armies. And while that fundamentally repressive strategy must be exposed and denounced, the reality is that the guerrilla strategy cannot lead to an assault on the power of the Colombian state. As the state becomes increasingly militarised, the space for mass democratic action will certainly become more restricted. But the imposition of the imperatives of globalisation is an absolute priority for the US. It is difficult to see how those imperatives can coexist for long with liberated territories of any kind. The domination of large areas by the paramilitaries, with the complicity of elements of the state, cannot coexist with a strengthened centralised power. The likely solution will be an attempt to incorporate the paramilitaries into the repressive state apparatus, while occasionally invoking human rights legislation against those who resist such incorporation. But elsewhere Colombia's human rights record will grow worse, since the priorities of Plan Colombia are deeply inconsistent with any regime of protection or defence of the rights of the majority. Defoliation of the coca fields does much more than kill coca bushes. It drives huge populations off the land, presumably also depriving the guerrillas of bases of support and emptying the terrain for easier occupation (and the experience of the 1960s provides the precedent). It may render the land ultimately safe for the oil and gas companies gazing lustfully at these areas. But the coca and the poppy will very soon be growing elsewhere—because the demand is there in the richer nations of the world, and the coca millions directly or indirectly flow into the restless capitals streaming through the international financial institutions.

Prediction in this situation is a dangerous procedure. One thing is sure, however. The deepening involvement of the US, through Plan Colombia, will not produce a modernisation that will in any way benefit the millions of displaced, exiled or terrorised Colombians who have expressed their resistance or despair in support for the guerrilla organisations (with possibly some 20,000 people under arms) or in their active involvement in a range of organisations of protest and resistance. In

Ecuador, in very recent times, the combined forces of workers' unions and indigenous organisations brought dramatic change and a real challenge to power. In Argentina the provisions of FTAA have met with furious and sustained resistance. The strategies of the revolutionary organisations must build on these successes—for if Latin America's political history has taught us anything, it is that no free territories will be allowed to exist in isolation for very long. They are crushed or they are absorbed by economic or military means. That is much harder to do when there are multiple fronts to fight on, and when the massed demonstrators of Genoa or Seattle seek the means of building active solidarity with all those who resist across the world.

Notes

1   US State Department website, www.state.gov/internatl
2   Foreign Office website, www.fco.gov.uk
3   J Petras, 'The Geopolitics of Plan Colombia', in *Monthly Review*, vol 53, no 1 (May 2001), p31.
4   US State Department website, op cit, 'International Information Programs', 30 June 2001. My emphasis.
5   See C Harding, *Colombia: A Guide to the People, Politics and Culture* (London, 1996), pp28-36. For a general discussion see J Pearce, *Colombia: Inside the Labyrinth* (London, 1990), ch 2.1, 'Colombia's Two Economies', and in particular pp103-115.
6   This was particularly true during the first period of government of Hugo Banzer, who became a millionaire several times over at this time. In his second manifestation, at the very end of the 1990s, Banzer became—in a twilight of life conversion—a vigorous advocate of suppressing the cultivation of coca. A grateful US government rewarded him with large amounts of aid and investment.
7   Escobar's story is most powerfully told by Gabriel García Márquez in his *News of a Kidnapping* (London, 1997).
8   This tension between regional and central power is a key to understanding Colombia's violent history.
9   W Tate, 'Repeating Past Mistakes', in *NACLA Report on the Americas,* vol XXXIV, no 2 (September-October 2000), p17.
10   R Vargas Meza, 'Biowarfare in Colombia?', in *NACLA Report on the Americas,* op cit, p21. My emphasis.
11   This conclusion of an OECD report is quoted in the document 'Plan Colombia: Máscaras y Artificios' by Belén Vásconez of the Comisión Ecuménica de Derechos Humanos of Ecuador, published on the web at www.pulsar.org.ec by the Pulsar Agency (27 November 2000).
12   Documented in convincing detail by R Vargas Meza, op cit.
13   For a general picture of that relationship Eduardo Galeano's classic *The Open Veins of Latin America* (New York, 1967) remains unsurpassed.
14   For a discussion of the moment of the revolution and its subsequent unfolding through the 1980s, see M Gonzalez, *Nicaragua: What Went Wrong?* (London, 1990).
15   J Petras and M Morley, *Latin America in a Time of Cholera* (London/New York, 1992), p63.

16   The Guatemalan peace accords would not finally be signed for another eight
      years.
17   Duncan Green's *The Silent Revolution* (London, 1995) is a painstaking and
      passionate account of the realities of that process.
18   These figures are quoted by R Vargas Meza in a fine piece called 'Plan Colombia:
      Construcción de Paz o Sobredosis de Guerra?' on the Equipo Nizkor website:
      www.derechos.org/nizkor/colombia/doc/vargas.html
19   It is interesting now to return to Jenny Pearce's characteristically thorough and
      insightful study, *Colombia: Inside the Labyrinth,* completed in 1989 and published
      the following year. She ends her book with this perspicacious question: 'Can an
      economy that has created only 500,000 jobs in manufacturing, which a leaked
      World Bank Report (July 1989) describes as closed and meeting the needs only of
      a minority, provide the majority of its population with a humane existence and the
      means to a livelihood? The archaic political order that has kept that minority in
      power has proved incapable of taking on this responsibility. The bomb will carry
      on ticking until it does, or until the left proves itself able to unite the people
      around an alternative social and political project' (p287).
20   See N Richani, 'The Paramilitary Connection', in *NACLA Report on the
      Americas,* op cit, pp38-41.
21   See G M Leech, 'The Drug War: an Exercise in Futility', in *Colombia Report* (16
      April 2001), www.colombiareport.org
22   See M Gonzalez, 'The Zapatistas: The Challenges of Revolution in the New
      Millennium', in *International Socialism* 89 (Winter 2000), pp59-80; and J Ross,
      The War Against Oblivion: The Zapatista Chronicles (Monroe, Maine, 2000).
23   J Petras, 'The Geopolitics of Plan Colombia', opcit, p35.
24   'Repeating Past Mistakes: Aiding Counterinsurgency in Colombia', *NACLA
      Report,* op cit, p17.
25   J Pearce, *Colombia: Inside the Labyrinth* (London, 1990), p47.
26   Ibid, pp49-68.
27   A fact reinforced by the recent capture of IRA members alleged to have gone to
      Colombia to train members of the FARC in the manufacture of bombs.
28   J Petras, op cit, p45. I suspect he is idealising somewhat here.

The new world recession

CHRIS HARMAN

> *The US is in the early stages of a recession which could be as deep and intractable as any since the Second World War, with serious consequences for the rest of the world.*

So wrote the dissident mainstream economist Wynne Godley in October.[1] Godley was one of the few economists predicting recession back in the giddy heights of the US stock exchange boom two years ago. But the forebodings are shared by many of a more conventional aspect. As Godley notes, 'Everyone agrees that the US now is in recession.'

Among those who agree is *The Economist*. Back in January it insisted that all the US faced was what it called a 'slowdown' or a 'correction'.[2] Now it says that 'there are good reasons to expect America's recession to be deeper and longer-lasting than most people expect... Indeed, it is possible that the world economy as a whole may be about to suffer its deepest downturn since the 1930s'.[3]

What has caused the turn around in opinion? And what is really happening to the world economy?

The crisis began well before the suicide hijack attack on the World Trade Centre on 11 September. The week before the attack the *Financial Times* had felt able to carry a three-part article on the crisis in the telecommunications industry which said, 'A \$1,000 billion bonfire of wealth has brought the world to the brink of recession'.[4] *The Economist* was just as pessimistic:

The sharp slowdown in America has already caused a recession, maybe not at home, but in Mexico, Singapore, Taiwan and elsewhere. In more and more countries around the world output is now stalling, if not falling. Total world output probably fell in the second quarter for the first time in two decades. Many commentators argue that America can still avoid recession, so long as consumer spending does not collapse. But 1982 suggests otherwise: America then had its deepest recession since the 1930s, yet consumer spending continued to grow, offset by plunging investment and exports.[5]

The roots of the crisis

I analysed the major elements in the US economy leading to recession in articles I wrote for this journal earlier this year,[6] and in *Socialist Review* early in 2000.[7] I only have room here to summarise the main points.

(i) The 'new economy', centred upon microchip-driven devices and telecommunications, did not alter the basic trajectory of the US economy. It increased productivity in certain sectors, but much less than the hype then suggested, and it could no more keep the boom going indefinitely than could the greater revolutionisation of production that had occurred in the 'new era' of the 'roaring' 1920s.

A recent report from the management research consultants McKinsey Global Institute confirms that:

In most sectors of the economy large increases in IT investment did not produce any improvement in productivity... Nearly all the post-1995 jump in productivity was in six sectors—retail, wholesale, securities, telecoms, semi-conductors and industrial machinery and equipment (mainly computers)...in the six sectors a number of factors contributed to the improvement—of which information technology was just one.[8]

(ii) The real driving force of the boom was a large-scale rationalisation of industry in response to the Japanese competitive challenge of the 1980s, combined with and based upon a massive increase in the rate of exploitation. Holding down wages and increasing working hours enabled the US ruling class to restore the rate of profit to roughly what it had been in the mid-1970s—although not to the higher level it had been at through the long boom from the 1940s to the 1970s.

(iii) The relatively rapid growth of the US economy compared with its major competitors attracted investable funds from all over the world. Stock exchange levels were driven ever higher, losing all contact with the real level of profitability in the economy. The ratio of share prices to dividends rose to more than twice its average over the previous 50 years.

At the same time, this inflow of funds made it possible for both firms and consumers to borrow on a massive scale, until total spending in the US exceeded total income by some 6 percent.

(iv) The boom had reached the point where it could only keep going if two contradictory things happened simultaneously—if profits were raised so as to justify share values, which meant further increasing the rate of exploitation, while wages were raised so as to sustain the level of consumption, which meant lowering the rate of exploitation. This underlying truth might be covered up for a period of months, but at some point the balloon was bound to be punctured. 'Capitalists…are so carried away by their own hype that they think the profits are magically going to rise. When these illusions are not fulfilled, the stock exchange, and probably the economy as whole, can only crash disastrously'.[9]

In fact, the situation was even worse than this. This runaway boom had led many firms to inflate their profits massively, so as to push up their share prices:

> *Spectacular growth in profits during the 1990s was partly due to dodgy accounting… According to Bob Barbera of Hoenig, an investment bank, the stated operating profits of the S&P 500 companies rose at a much faster rate than the share of profits measured in the national accounts… Thus, in the 1990s, profits at S&P 500 companies tripled, but profits recorded in the national accounts merely doubled.*
>
> *Whether technology-industry profits actually grew as fast in recent years as they appeared to do is increasingly being questioned. A recent study by Gary Schieneman, Steven Milunovich and Lisa Liu, all analysts at Merrill Lynch, examined 37 leading technology companies. The study found that accounting properly for options and non-operating expenses reduced the firms' profits by 25 percent on average.*[10]

This suggests that profitability through the economy as a whole in the late 1990s was, in fact, considerably less than that of the pre-crisis years of the early 1970s and closer to the considerably lower levels of the 1980s.[11]

The turn from boom to bust

A boom of sorts did keep going through the first nine months of 2001 on both sides of the Atlantic. It was a boom in consumption even while core industries began to sack workers and to announce falls in profits, leading to a slow but cumulatively sizeable fall in share prices. Hence the talk in the summer of 'two economies'—still booming service and personal consumption sectors, and increasingly depressed manufacturing and industrial sectors.

The economic importance of 11 September was that, at least in the US, it burst the consumption balloon. It also provided industrial firms with a smokescreen behind which they could massively speed up their announcements about poor profits and their sacking of workers.

Both these things would have happened anyway. As *The Observer* reported on 23 September:

> *It was clear from the hundreds of profits warnings that corporate America has decided to announce all of its bad news at once. Honeywell International third-quarter profits would be between 43 cents and 45 cents a share, compared with 76 cents last year. The company is now considering cutting 12,000 jobs… Eastman Kodak said that third-quarter profits would be a third below estimates. Levis said it was cutting production as sales had fallen on last year. American Express saw its share price fall to its lowest level since the Asian crisis.*
>
> *Analysts predict more bad news. 'We're looking at something more than a 20 percent decline in earnings for the S&P 500 compared with the same quarter last year,' said Chuck Hill, a director of Thomson Financial, the research company that tracks corporate profits.*[12]

The Guardian repeated the same point some days later:

> *Companies are now taking long-overdue action to reduce their costs and boost their earnings, which they are doing by taking advantage of the terrorist attacks to sack their employees in droves. A study conducted by leading economists in the US has found that the airline and hotel industries have laid off tens of thousands of workers since 11 September.*
>
> *Professor Christopher Thornberg, of the University of California, Los Angeles, said airlines had been bleeding red, losing money hand over fist. They needed to get rid of employees… Now the airlines say 'the devil made me do it. Bin Laden—he's the one who made me lay off these people'.*
>
> *He added that the tourist trade was also in trouble before the attacks. Occupancy rates had fallen from 63 percent to 55 percent during the summer, he said. Now they had an excuse to lay off workers without fearing any industrial difficulties.*[13]

By late October the *Financial Times* could report:

> *The terrorist attacks have had less impact on companies' costs and strategy than expected, according to the chief executives of the biggest US companies. But big business is reeling from the effects of a recession that most executives*

believe was already under way.[14]

This is an important point, because many supporters of capitalism have attempted to blame each recession of the last 27 years on extraneous events. For instance, there are frequent claims (in *The Guardian* and elsewhere) that the recession of the early 1990s was caused by an increase in the price of oil resulting from the Gulf War. In fact the average price of oil through the years 1990 and 1991 was no higher than it had been previously. It shot up for a month or two and then fell just as sharply. The recession followed from the internal dynamics of capitalism, particularly in the industrial countries, not from some external factor. The same is true of the present recession.

The stock exchanges and the real economy

The most dramatic effects of the destruction of the twin towers was on the level of US share prices. The Dow Jones industrial average fell 684.81 points on the first day stock exchanges reopened.[15] Two days later the *Financial Times* spoke of:

> *...one of the worst bear markets in history. In early trading yesterday, the Dow Jones Industrial Average had fallen 31 percent from its January 2000 peak, one of the worst ten declines the US market has experienced since the First World War. In Germany, the DAX index has more than halved since the peak in March 2000; in London, the FTSE 100 has fallen 36 percent since its peak in December 1999.*[16]

Stock exchange levels are of central importance to whole sections of the capitalist class. They determine the cash value of the shares they own and the stock options that come with directorships of companies. But the exchanges do not play anything like the same central role in terms of the dynamics of the system such people preside over. Relatively little new investment is raised through stock exchanges. Their main function is in providing a market place for the buying and selling of shares in already-existing companies. They are, in fact, secondhand markets, whose relationship with the main business of capitalism—the accumulation of surplus value through exploitation at the point of production—is somewhat analogous to that of used car dealers to the activities of the giant car manufacturers.

A collapse of stock exchange levels sometimes indicates something fundamentally wrong with the system as whole, and a rise in the levels sometimes suggests the system is enjoying better health. What is more, a sudden collapse in the share values of some companies can do a lot of damage to the balance sheets of other companies and financial institutions that have tried to raise their own profitability by gambling on them. But there is no automatic correlation between the ups and downs of the stock markets and the ups and downs of the real economy. So, for instance, the Dow fell 40 percent between 1939 and 1942, in the early stages of the Second World War—just as US capitalism was entering one of the biggest booms it had known.

This time round the lack of direct correlation between the stock markets and the real economy was shown within a matter of a couple of weeks. For, while the real economy continued heading into recession, with mass sacking and more reports of low profits, the US and British stock exchanges started rising!

The Guardian reported:

> There was a whiff of the good times returning to Wall Street yesterday with share prices ending back to where they were before September 11.
>
> After the massive falls in share prices in the immediate aftermath of the devastation in New York and Washington, markets have roared back on both sides of the Atlantic. London's FTSE 100 index is now higher than it was before 11 September, and at one point yesterday the technology rich Nasdaq was within five points of its levels before 11 September…while the price earnings ratio for the S&P 500 is back to its levels before the hi-tech crash 18 months ago.[17]

It is a proof of how short-sighted capitalists can be that they celebrated such a return to the old ratio of share prices to dividends. That ratio, as we have seen, was twice its historic average and was based on completely unfulfillable expectations about massive increases in profit levels. It was nonsensical then. It is even more nonsensical now, with virtually every company looking at reduced profit levels.

In fact the damage the recession was causing to the real economy was escalating all the time. Two days after this report *The Guardian* told:

> Bethlehem (the steel corporation) filed for protection against its creditors yesterday in the US. This is the company that brought us much of the raw material for the Empire State Building. One cannot help but notice how many iconic names of America's corporate past are now tumbling into insolvency courts. Last week saw Polaroid file under America's Chapter 11. Bethlehem Steel will not be the last great American name to go to the wall before the year is out.[18]

Ten days later:

> Investors sold stocks and the dollar after disastrous data from the US…

Orders for durable goods, which most economists expected to show a small decline, sank 8.5 percent in September. The weekly totals of new claims for jobless benefits in the US rose to 504,000, the four-week moving average hitting its highest since the depths of the recession in 1991.[19]

The debt overhang

Numerous companies—in Britain as well as in the US—borrowed frenetically in an attempt to cash in on the boom two to three years ago. Now many are very close to going bust, with profits which barely cover their debt repayments. They only have to miss one payment for their creditworthiness to collapse, other firms to call in their debts and the receivers to come knocking on the door—quite likely in the company of the fraud squad. This is what happened to such celebrated business figures as Robert Maxwell and Asil Nadir in the recession of the early 1990s. It could happen to any one of a number of big names this time round.

The most obviously overstretched firms are those that rushed into the new technology sector associated with microchips, computers, telecoms and the internet. In Britain the one time engineering giant Marconi-GEC has only just survived a meltdown in its value. It is common knowledge that the cable firms Telewest and NTL are in a very tight situation and that the terrestrial television companies of the ITV network are doing very badly. But the damage is not confined to these sectors as the following list of most indebted British companies suggests:[20]

FINANCIAL STRENGTH INDEX (100 = WORST IN EUROPE)

Telewest	*97*
British Airways	*96*
BskyB	*93.7*
United Utilities	*90*
Powergen	*90*
Railtrack	*89.7*
British Telecom	*89.7*
Lattice	*86.7*
Invensys	*85.3*
Scottish Power	*83.7*

A sudden decline in advertising has already hit the magazine publishing sector very hard, while the travel industry was in trouble even before the collapse of US tourism after 11 September. The troubles of the airlines (Virgin and BA) and aero manufacturers were rooted as much as those of the internet companies in the mania of the boom years. And in other sectors many managing directors will be trying to bluff it out, knowing that one small push could knock them over.

Economics to politics

The transition from boom to recession is never a smooth, evenly balanced decline. There are always some firms that gamble more heavily than others during the boom. There are always some industries hit disproportionately hard by the downturn. So periods of apparently smooth decline are always interspersed with sudden crises when giant firms and even whole industries are suddenly on the verge of collapse. And as quantity turns into quality, so economic collapse can suddenly cause political eruptions. Governments find it difficult to do nothing as they are faced with the desperate demands of giant capitalists and the sudden bitterness of large numbers of workers. But whatever they do—even if they do nothing—brings to the surface considerations about the whole direction of society.

Through the early autumn 11 September and then the war against Afghanistan diverted people's attention from the harm the recession was doing. This is unlikely to continue as the winter wears on.

Some of the problems are already coming to the surface in the US. The Bush administration rushed to pump in government money to deal with the immediate shock caused by the destruction of the twin towers. The *Financial Times* reports:

This week, with little ceremony, President George W Bush quietly brought to a close more than a decade of US economic policy orthodoxy. By signalling support for lower taxes and higher public spending in the next year that could reach as high as $130bn—1.3 percent of gross domestic product—he threw the US administration's weight behind the proposition that a temporary deficiency in aggregate demand should be met by a shift in government finances from surplus to deficit.

This argument, the simplest distillation of the teachings of John Maynard Keynes, has been out of favour in much of the industrialised world for ten years or more. But with the world's three largest economies—the US, Japan and Germany—all in recession or close to it, the conventional wisdom is up for reassessment.

In the US, the intellectual climate has shifted decisively in favour of just such an activist policy. In the rest of the world, however, a revival of Keynesianism is still viewed with suspicion.

The conversion of Mr Bush and his Republican Party to the cause of fiscal stimulus has been going on for some months. But it has taken the tragedies of 11 September and their potentially devastating economic consequences to complete the process.[21]

   Even the Federal Reserve has joined in the calls for an activist fiscal policy [with] *Alan Greenspan telling members of Congress that a total stimulus of about 1 percent of gross domestic product would be prudent.*[22]

This revival of Keynesian methods of state intervention is being greeted in some quarters as a welcome move that can see off the crisis. It can correct, it is said, the damage done by reliance on free market capitalism and even represent the end of neo-liberalism. Such, for instance, is the tone of some of the coverage in *The Guardian.*

The inadequacy of Keynesian solutions

But Keynesian methods cannot deal with the fundamental imbalances in the US economy that developed in the boom of the late 1990s. Investment in key industries far outstripped any increase in the source of profits. The current fall in profit rates is the inevitable consequence.

   The rate of profit cannot be restored without, on the one hand, further massive restructuring of industry through large numbers of firms going to the wall and, on the other, a huge increase in the rate of exploitation by slashing workforces and cutting wages—as is already happening in the airline, aerospace and hotel industries. But in the short term such measures can only lead to a deepening of the crisis and a further fall in consumption, with ricochet effects right across the economy. Firms and private consumers will be under pressure to cut back desperately in order to try to get out of debt (or to end their 'negative saving' as some economists describe it). But it was precisely their borrowing that kept the US economy from sinking completely before 11 September.

   Wynne Godley describes the likely consequences of them ending their indebtedness:

   If private net saving reverts to its historic norm over the next two years this would remove a gigantic chunk of demand equal to about 7 to 8 percent of GDP, or $750bn, from the circular flow of income. Such a deficiency would swamp all the announced expansionary fiscal measures, which can hardly exceed $100- 200bn per annum at the outside.[23]

In other words the recession is bringing to an end the orgy of borrowing that has kept consumption and investment flowing until recently. The resulting decline in markets is likely to be between four and eight times greater than any stimulus to the market coming from changes in US government policy so far.

   Yet there are already doubts in the US ruling class as to whether even that level of stimulus is desirable. The stimulus is meant to come from an excess of government expenditure over tax revenues. The Republicans want to achieve this by further tax cuts. The Democrats in Congress are arguing that this will lead to an excessive demand for funds from money markets, so leading to such a rise in long term interest rates as to further reduce private investment:

> *Democrats argue, the damage to the economy from such a fiscal policy is not confined to the effect on interest rates, says Robert Rubin, the former Treasury secretary, 'The more important factor is confidence. Once you lose control of your fiscal affairs it creates a general loss of confidence in economic management'.*[24]

Some of the Democrats are simply using the argument as a way of pushing their preferred stimulus to the economy, through increased public spending, as an alternative to the Republicans' tax cuts. But, whatever their motives, they are pointing to the central problem from a capitalist point of view. Even the limited Keynesian budgetary measures proposed so far will run into serious problems in the medium term. Any improvement in profits due to their effect in expanding the demand for goods is going to be countered by the effect on profits and capitalist confidence of the government borrowing that provides for that demand. What they gain on the swings they are likely to lose on the roundabouts.

This was exactly the problem Keynes himself confronted—and ran away from—in the 1930s. Every proposal he made, notes Skidelsky in his biography, was tailored, 'taking into account the psychology of the business community. In practice he was very cautious indeed'.[25] In practice neither the British nor the US governments intervened on the scale needed to deal with that crisis until they established a centrally directed war economy. Despite the tone of the bellicose rhetoric coming from sections of the Bush administration we are not going to see that in the near future. The US state will take measures to protect giant US firms. US governments have usually been careful not to let the neo-liberal ideology they propagate through the rest of the world hurt domestic businesses too much and have been quite happy to use the state to bolster and restructure US capitalism. But there is no sign of a stimulus on anything like the scale pessimists such as Wynne Godley see as necessary.

What does this mean for Britain?

The official prognosis is that the British economy is strong enough to escape virtually unharmed from the world recession, since interest rates are low, inflation is low and projected increases in government spending should compensate for any reduction in foreign markets. Such glib optimism ignores a few elementary points. The British economy, like the US economy until recently, has been kept afloat by consumer spending. Overall borrowing by households rose by 10 percent last year, the highest level since 1991. It is doubtful whether that rise will continue if the surge of redundancies we've seen in recent months continues. And more redundancies are likely, since 'company profitability has fallen to its lowest level in five and a half years, raising fears that businesses are set to shed more jobs and cut investment to claw back disappearing margins'.[26]

At the same time, the other side of the consumer boom has been an increasing excess of imports over exports. This can be sustained so long as the belief persists that British capitalism is doing better than its European, US and Japanese competitors, leading to an inflow of international funds. But should any doubts begin to rise about this, the flow could reverse overnight, suddenly creating a great sense of crisis. A couple of years back there was a strong current of mainstream opinion arguing for a reduction in the value of the pound against the euro, on the grounds that this would increase the competitiveness of manufacturing industry. But when the value of the pound began, briefly, to fall in the summer there were sudden worries that this would be counterproductive. A lower pound would not succeed in raising the volume of exports as much as necessary should world trade stagnate (and some estimates suggest it will only grow by about 2 percent in the coming year),[27] but would reduce the sterling value of each item sold: 'The decline in sterling against the dollar and the Euro could hammer manufacturers further. Economists said slack global demand may negate any competitive advantage from a weaker pound'.[28]

New Labour has had a fair degree of economic luck over the last four years. It is unlikely to be enough to stop Britain being sucked into the global recession. And, although this is unlikely to worry born again Blairites all that much, the avalanche of jobs losses is likely to get worse.

The war and the recession

The effects of the US's resort to war have been contradictory. On the one hand, the US military has been able to pump money into certain industries and provide them with a floor below which markets will not fall—especially as Bush is finding it easier to push the Son of Star Wars programme through. On the other hand, the sense of instability can further damage the confidence of businesses and consumers.

What is important here is not, in the main, what happens on the military front—although what happens next in Afghanistan, and any extension to the war elsewhere (for instance in Iraq), will make a difference. Most significant will be whatever happens in the wide region stretching from the Nile to the Indus.

War often leads to political instability culminating in revolutions. But it is not often that the potential for revolutionary upheaval affecting their vital interests worries rulers when a war is only a few weeks old. But that has been a constraining factor on the US administration's conduct of its military operations. Media commentators talk openly of the possibility of revolutionary upheavals in countries such as Saudi Arabia and Egypt, and they fear the impact of the war on Afghanistan on the festering conflict between India and Pakistan over Kashmir.

But there are powerful currents within the administration which are dismissive of such fears as they push to broaden the military actions so as to achieve wider US global objectives. It is impossible to tell who will win out, or how close to revolutionary upheaval places like Saudi Arabia really are. But there can be no doubting the devastating impact on the US economy if a widening of the war were to result in the sweeping away of any of the regimes that guard the US's oil supplies.

Meanwhile, the deepening of the recession will increase instability in many different parts of the world. In Europe it is likely to accentuate the trend we saw in the early 1990s and summed up as 'the 1930s in slow motion'—a polarisation away from the centre towards the forces both of the far right and of a revived left. The important change since the early 1990s is the growth of the anti-capitalist movement, usually now central in the anti-war movements. It can provide a focus for the sudden bitterness created by the crisis in a way which was hardly possible a decade ago.

In parts of the Third World we may well see 'the 1930s in fast motion'—economic crisis on such a scale as to destabilise old political formations and states that depend on them.

'Private capital flows to emerging economies will fall sharply, producing the toughest financial conditions for these countries since the debt crises of the 1980s', warned the Institute of International Finance, a body representing global banks and asset managers, in September. It expected developing country exports to decline by 2 percent this year after growing by 22 percent in 2000.[29]

How desperate things could get was shown in Argentina long before 11 September. The government was thrown into crisis in the spring as it attempted to make massive cuts to the educational budget after three years of recession. It bought time for itself by giving the economic portfolio to Domingo Cavallo, who had been economics minister for the government thrown out at the previous election. He was briefly hailed in the media as the nation's saviour. By the summer he was having to push through his own even more savage package of cuts in return for an $8 billion IMF loan. Yet the economy continued sliding:

> *Argentina's economic recession, now in its fourth year, seems to be deepening. Construction activity fell 11 percent in August compared with the previous year while industrial production fell almost 6 percent.*
>
> *September car production sagged 47 percent compared with a year ago. Consumer confidence is now close to historic lows. The immediate consequence is that tax collection plummeted 14 percent in September, forcing the government into yet another of round of spending cuts to meet its zero-deficit target.[30]*

The government, not surprisingly, received a thrashing in provincial elections in October. In Buenos Aires, where a huge chunk of the electorate cast blank votes, the opposition Peronists got a majority of seats, but a quarter of votes went to the various parties of the far left. Against such a background it is hardly surprising that most commentators think it can only be a matter of time before the government is forced to devalue its currency and default on some of its debts.

Such a course might bring some revival to the Argentinian economy. But its impact internationally could be devastating. The country 'accounts for more than 20 percent of the emerging market bond index'.[31] Default would damage those (mainly US) banks which have lent to Argentina—and would lead others to withdraw funds from other countries, so pushing them to the brink of bankruptcy. Some are in the zone subject to all the aftershocks of the Afghan war. Turkey has vied with Argentina for a year as the state which most worries the financiers. Egypt is deep in debt, despite some writing off of what it owed ten years ago as a bribe for backing the US war against Iraq. Pakistan owes $37 billion, but the debt relief bribe on offer so far is meagre. At present no less than 60 percent of Pakistan government revenues go on servicing its debt—under the proposed rescheduling scheme this would only fall to 50 percent.[32] And all these countries' exports will be hit by the downturn in American, Japanese and European economies.

This definitely means increased poverty for very large numbers of people. It remains to be seen whether that will translate into the eruption of mass bitterness on the streets and the toppling of governments. But it certainly shortens the odds on this happening.

The official prognosis from apologists for the world's ruling classes is that a short recession will 'correct' the excesses of the boom years, and that a quick military victory will dispose of the threat to the US's client regimes in the Middle East.

If this is how things turn out, they will be very lucky indeed. Bush and Blair have unleashed war that can have all sorts of unpredictable consequences in a region that is full of highly combustible material at a time when their economies are skidding all over the place.

Notes

1   Reprinted as 'Recession, USA' in *The Guardian*, 23 October 2001.
2   *The Economist*, 6 January 2001.
3   *The Economist*, 20 October 2001.
4   *Financial Times*, 5 September 2001
5   *The Economist*, 25 August 2001.
6   See C Harman, 'Beyond the Boom', *International Socialism* 90 (Spring 2001).
7   See C Harman, 'Paradigm Lost', *Socialist Review*, February 2000, and C Harman, 'Life in the Fast Lane', *Socialist Review*, April 2000.
8   Precis of report in *Financial Times*, 17 October 2001.
9   C Harman, 'Beyond the Boom', op cit.
10 *The Economist*, 23 June 2001.
11 Firms also inflated profits in the boom of those years. For details, see my 'Where is Capitalism Going?', *International Socialism* 58 (Spring 1993).
12 *The Observer*, 23 September 2001.
13 *The Guardian*, 12 October 2001.
14 *Financial Times*, 26 October 2001.
15 *Financial Times*, 20 September 2001.
16 *Financial Times*, 22 September 2001.
17 *The Guardian*, 12 October 2001.
18 *The Guardian*, 16 October 2001.
19 *Financial Times*, 26 January 2001.
20 ABN Amro figures, given in *The Guardian*, 6 October 2001.
21 *Financial Times*, 6 October 2001.
22 *Financial Times*, 16 October 2001.
23 'Recession, USA', op cit.
24 *Financial Times*, 16 October 2001.
25 For a fuller discussion on this with sources, see C Harman, 'The Crisis of Bourgeois Economics', *International Socialism* 71 (Summer 1996).
26 *Financial Times*, 6 October 2001.
27 See, for instance, the World Trade Organisation estimate, reported in *Financial Times*, 26 October 2001.
28 *Financial Times*, 12 June 2001.
29 *Financial Times*, 21 September 2001.
30 *Financial Times*, 9 October 2001.
31 *Financial Times*, 25 August 2001.
32 *Financial Times*, 30 October 2001.

The Socialist Workers Party is one of an international grouping of socialist organisations:

AUSTRALIA	International Socialists, PO Box A338, Sydney South
AUSTRIA	Linkswende, Postfach 87, 1108 Wien
BRITAIN	Socialist Workers Party, PO Box 82, London E3 3LH
CANADA	International Socialists, PO Box 339, Station E, Toronto, Ontario M6H 4E3
CYPRUS	Ergatiki Demokratia, PO Box 7280, Nicosia
CZECH REPUBLIC	Socialisticka Solidarita, PO Box 1002, 11121 Praha 1
DENMARK	Internationale Socialister, PO Box 5113, 8100 Aarhus C
GERMANY	Linksruck, Postfach 304 183, 20359 Hamburg
GREECE	Sosialistiko Ergatiko Komma, c/o Workers Solidarity, PO Box 8161, Athens 100 10
HOLLAND	Internationale Socialisten, PO Box 92025, 1090AA Amsterdam
IRELAND	Socialist Workers Party, PO Box 1648, Dublin 8
NEW ZEALAND	Socialist Workers Organization, PO Box 13-685, Auckland
NORWAY	Internasjonale Socialisterr, Postboks 9226 Grønland, 0134 Oslo
POLAND	Pracownicza Demokracja, PO Box 12, 01-900 Warszawa 118
SPAIN	Izquierda Revolucionaria, Apartado 563, 08080 Barcelona
UNITED STATES	Left Turn, PO Box 445, New York, NY 10159-0445
ZIMBABWE	International Socialist Organisation, PO Box 6758, Harare

The following issues of *International Socialism* (second series) are available price £3 (including postage) from IS Journal, PO Box 82, London E3 3LH. *International Socialism* 2:58 and 2:65 are available on cassette from the Royal National Institute for the Blind (Peterborough Library Unit). Phone 01733 370 777.

International Socialism 2:92 Autumn 2001

Tom Behan: 'Nothing can be the same again' ★ Boris Kagarlitsky: The road from Genoa ★ Alex Callinicos: Toni Negri in perspective ★ Jack Fuller: The new workerism: the politics of the Italian autonomists ★ Goretti Horgan: How does globalisation affect women? ★ Rumy Hasan: East Asia since the 1997 crisis ★ Charlie Kimber: Dark heart of imperialism ★ Megan Trudell: The pursuit of 'unbounded freedom' ★

International Socialism 2:91 Summer 2001

Susan George: What now? ★ Walden Bello: The global conjuncture ★ Chris Nineham: An idea whose time has come ★ Mike Marqusee: Labour's long march to the right ★ Mike Davis: Wild streets—*American Graffiti* versus the Cold War ★ Goretti Horgan: Changing women's lives in Ireland ★ John Lister: We will fight them in the hedgerows ★ Mike Gonzalez: The Zapatistas after the Great March—a postscript ★ Dragan Plavsic: Hoist on their own petards ★

International Socialism 2:90 Spring 2001

John Rees: Anti-capitalism, reformism and socialism ★ Chris Harman: Beyond the boom ★ Walden Bello: 2000: the year of global protest ★ Michael Lavalette and others: The woeful record of the House of Blair ★ Brian Manning: History and socialism ★ Peter Morgan: A troublemaker's charter ★

International Socialism 2:89 Winter 2000

Lindsey German: Serbia's spring in October ★ Anne Alexander: Powerless in Gaza: the Palestinian Authority and the myth of the 'peace process' ★ Boris Kagarlitsky: The lessons of Prague ★ Mike Gonzalez: The Zapatistas: the challenges of revolution in a new millennium ★ Stuart Hood: Memoirs of the Italian Resistance ★ Esme Choonara: Threads of resistance ★ Megan Trudell: Setting the record straight ★ Judy Cox: Reasons to be cheerful: theories of anti-capitalism ★ Mark O'Brien: A comment on *Tailism and the Dialectic* ★

International Socialism 2:88 Autumn 2000

Chris Harman: Anti-capitalism: theory and practice ★ Paul McGarr: Why green is red ★ Boris Kagarlitsky: The suicide of *New Left Review* ★ Gilbert Achcar: The 'historical pessimism' of Perry Anderson ★ Dave Renton: Class consciousness and the origins of Labour ★ Keith Flett: Socialists and the origins of Labour: some other perspectives ★ John Newsinger: Fantasy and revolution: an interview with China Miéville ★

International Socialism 2:87 Summer 2000

Lindsey German: How Labour lost its roots ★ Mark O'Brien: Socialists and the origins of Labour ★ Judy Cox: Skinning a live tiger paw by paw ★ Peter Morgan: The morning after the night before... ★ John Newsinger: Plumbing the depths: some recent books on New Labour ★ Abbie Bakan: From Seattle to Washington: the making of a movement ★ Jim Wolfreys: In perspective: Pierre Bourdieu ★ Nick Barrett: Complement to 'Reformism and class polarisation in Europe' ★ Mark Krantz: Humanitarian intentions on the road to hell ★ John Rees: Tony Cliff: theory and practice ★ Ygal Sarneh: A revolutionary life ★ Shaun Doherty: The language of liberation ★

International Socialism 2:86 Spring 2000

John Charlton: Talking Seattle ★ Abbie Bakan: After Seattle: the politics of the World Trade Organisation ★ Mark O'Brien: In perspective: Susan George ★ Rob Ferguson: Chechnya: the empire strikes back ★ Lindsey German: The Balkans' imperial problem ★ Megan Trudell: The Russian civil war: a Marxist analysis ★ Robin Blackburn: Reviewing the millennia ★ Jim Wolfreys: In defence of Marxism ★ Judy Cox: Can capitalism be sustained? ★

International Socialism 2:85 Winter 1999

Alex Callinicos: Reformism and class polarisation in Europe ★ Michael Lavalette and Gerry Mooney: New Labour, new moralism: the welfare politics and ideology of New Labour under Blair ★ Ken Coates: Benign imperialism versus United Nations ★ John Baxter: Is the UN an alternative to 'humanitarian imperialism'? ★ John Rose: Jesus: history's most famous missing person ★ Chris Harman: The 20th century: an age of extremes or an age of possibilities? ★ Mike Gonzalez: Is modernism dead? ★ Peter Morgan: The man behind the mask ★ Anne Alexander: All power to the imagination ★ Anna Chen: George Orwell: a literary Trotskyist? ★ Rob Hoveman: History of theory ★ Chris Harman: Comment on Molyneux on art ★

International Socialism 2:84 Autumn 1999
Neil Davidson: The trouble with 'ethnicity' ★ Jim Wolfreys: Class struggles in France ★ Phil Marfleet: Nationalism and internationalism ★ Tom Behan: The return of Italian Communism ★ Andy Durgan: Freedom fighters or Comintern army? The International Brigades in Spain ★ John Molyneux: Art, alienation and capitalism: a reply to Chris Nineham ★ Judy Cox: Dreams of equality: the levelling poor of the English Revolution ★

International Socialism 2:83 Summer 1999
John Rees: The socialist revolution and the democratic revolution ★ Mike Haynes: Theses on the Balkan War ★ Angus Calder: Into slavery: the rise of imperialism ★ Jim Wolfreys: The physiology of barbarism ★ John Newsinger: Scenes from the class war: Ken Loach and socialist cinema ★

International Socialism 2:82 Spring 1999
Lindsey German: The Blair project cracks ★ Dan Atkinson and Larry Elliott: Reflating Keynes: a different view of the crisis ★ Peter Morgan: The new Keynesians: staking a hold in the system? ★ Rob Hoveman: Brenner and crisis: a critique ★ Chris Nineham: Art and alienation: a reply to John Molyneux ★ Paul McGarr: Fascists brought to book ★ Brian Manning: Revisionism revised ★ Neil Davidson: In perspective: Tom Nairn ★

International Socialism 2:81 Winter 1998
Alex Callinicos: World capitalism at the abyss ★ Mike Haynes and Pete Glatter: The Russian catastrophe ★ Phil Marfleet: Globalisation and the Third World ★ Lindsey German: In a class of its own ★ Judy Cox: John Reed: reporting on the revolution ★ Kevin Ovenden: The resistible rise of Adolf Hitler ★

International Socialism 2:80 Autumn 1998
Clare Fermont: Indonesia: the inferno of revolution ★ Workers' representatives and socialists: Three interviews from Indonesia ★ Chris Bambery: Report from Indonesia ★ Tony Cliff: Revolution and counter-revolution: lessons for Indonesia ★ John Molyneux: The legitimacy of modern art ★ Gary McFarlane: A respectable trade? Slavery and the rise of capitalism ★ Paul McGarr: The French Revolution: Marxism versus capitalism ★ Shaun Doherty: Will the real James Connolly please stand up? ★

International Socialism 2:79 Summer 1998
John Rees: The return of Marx? ★ Lindsey German: Reflections on *The Communist Manifesto* ★ Judy Cox: An introduction to Marx's theory of alienation ★ Judith Orr: Making a comeback: the Marxist theory of crisis ★ Megan Trudell: New Labour, old conflicts: the story so far ★ John Molyneux: State of the art ★ Anna Chen: In perspective: Sergei Eisenstein ★ Jonathan Neale: Vietnam veterans ★ Phil Gasper: Bookwatch: Marxism and science ★

International Socialism 2:78 Spring 1998
Colin Sparks: The eye of the storm ★ Shin Gyoung-hee: The crisis and the workers' movement in South Korea ★ Rob Hoveman: Financial crises and the real economy ★ Peter Morgan: Class divisions in the gay community ★ Alex Callinicos: The secret of the dialectic ★ John Parrington: It's life, Jim, but not as we know it ★ Judy Cox: Robin Hood: earl, outlaw or rebel? ★ Ian Birchall: The vice-like hold of nationalism? A comment on Megan Trudell's 'Prelude to revolution' ★ William Keach: In perspective: Alexander Cockburn and Christopher Hitchens ★

International Socialism 2:77 Winter 1997
Audrey Farrell: Addicted to profit—capitalism and drugs ★ Mike Gonzalez: The resurrections of Che Guevara ★ Sam Ashman: India: imperialism, partition and resistance ★ Henry Maitles: Never again! ★ John Baxter: The return of political science ★ Dave Renton: Past its peak ★

International Socialism 2:76 Autumn 1997
Mike Haynes: Was there a parliamentary alternative in 1917? ★ Megan Trudell: Prelude to revolution: class consciousness and the First World War ★ Judy Cox: A light in the darkness ★ Pete Glatter: Victor Serge: writing for the future ★ Gill Hubbard: A guide to action ★ Chris Bambery: Review article: Labour's history of hope and despair ★

International Socialism 2:75 Summer 1997
John Rees: The class struggle under New Labour ★ Alex Callinicos: Europe: the mounting crisis ★ Lance Selfa: Mexico after the Zapatista uprising ★ William Keach: Rise like lions? Shelley and the revolutionary left ★ Judy Cox: What state are we really in? ★ John Parrington: In perspective: Valentin Voloshinov ★

International Socialism 2:73 Winter 1996
Chris Harman: Globalisation: a critique of a new orthodoxy ★ Chris Bambery: Marxism and sport ★ John Parrington: Computers and consciousness: a reply to Alex Callinicos ★ Joe Faith: Dennett, materialism and empiricism ★ Megan Trudell: Who made the American Revolution? ★ Mark O'Brien: The class conflicts which shaped British history ★ John Newsinger: From class war to Cold War ★ Alex Callinicos: The state in debate ★ Charlie Kimber: Review article: coming to terms with barbarism in Rwanda in Burundi ★

International Socialism 2:72 Autumn 1996
Alex Callinicos: Betrayal and discontent: Labour under Blair ★ Sue Cockerill and Colin Sparks: Japan in crisis ★ Richard Levins: When science fails us ★ Ian Birchall: The Babeuf bicentenary: conspiracy or revolutionary party? ★ Brian Manning: A voice for the poor ★ Paul O'Flinn: From the kingdom of necessity to the kingdom of freedom: Morris's *News from Nowhere* ★ Clare Fermont: Bookwatch: Palestine and the Middle East 'peace process' ★

International Socialism 2:71 Summer 1996
Chris Harman: The crisis of bourgeois economics ★ Hassan Mahamdallie: William Morris and revolutionary Marxism ★ Alex Callinicos: Darwin, materialism and revolution ★ Chris Nineham: Raymond Williams: revitalising the left? ★ Paul Foot: A passionate prophet of liberation ★ Gill Hubbard: Why has feminism failed women? ★ Lee Sustar: Bookwatch: fighting to unite black and white ★

International Socialism 2:70 Spring 1996
Alex Callinicos: South Africa after apartheid ★ Chris Harman: France's hot December ★ Brian Richardson: The making of a revolutionary ★ Gareth Jenkins: Why Lucky Jim turned right—an obituary of Kingsley Amis ★ Mark O'Brien: The bloody birth of capitalism ★ Lee Humber: Studies in revolution ★ Adrian Budd: A new life for Lenin ★ Martin Smith: Bookwatch: the General Strike ★

International Socialism 2:69 Winter 1995
Lindsey German: The Balkan war: can there be peace? ★ Duncan Blackie: The left and the Balkan war ★ Nicolai Gentchev: The myth of welfare dependency ★ Judy Cox: Wealth, poverty and class in Britain today ★ Peter Morgan: Trade unions and strikes ★ Julie Waterson: The party at its peak ★ Megan Trudell: Living to some purpose ★ Nick Howard: The rise and fall of socialism in one city ★ Andy Durgan: Bookwatch: Civil war and revolution in Spain ★

International Socialism 2:68 Autumn 1995
Ruth Brown: Racism and immigration in Britain ★ John Molyneux: Is Marxism deterministic? ★ Stuart Hood: News from nowhere? ★ Lee Sustar: Communism in the heart of the beast ★ Peter Linebaugh: To the teeth and forehead of our faults ★ George Paizis: Back to the future ★ Phil Marshall: The children of stalinism ★ Paul D'Amato: Bookwatch: 100 years of cinema ★

International Socialism 2:67 Summer 1995
Paul Foot: When will the Blair bubble burst? ★ Chris Harman: From Bernstein to Blair—100 years of revisionism ★ Chris Bambery: Was the Second World War a war for democracy? ★ Alex Callinicos: Hope against the Holocaust ★Chris Nineham: Is the media all powerful? ★ Peter Morgan: How the West was won ★ Charlie Hore: Bookwatch: China since Mao ★

International Socialism 2:66 Spring 1995
Dave Crouch: The crisis in Russia and the rise of the right ★ Phil Gasper: Cruel and unusual punishment: the politics of crime in the United States ★ Alex Callinicos: Backwards to liberalism ★ John Newsinger: Matewan: film and working class struggle ★ John Rees: The light and the dark ★ Judy Cox: How to make the Tories disappear ★ Charlie Hore: Jazz: a reply to the critics ★ Pat Riordan: Bookwatch: Ireland ★

International Socialism 2:65 Special issue
Lindsey German: Frederick Engels: life of a revolutionary ★ John Rees: Engels' Marxism ★ Chris Harman: Engels and the origins of human society ★ Paul McGarr: Engels and natural science ★

International Socialism 2:63 Summer 1994
Alex Callinicos: Crisis and class struggle in Europe today ★ Duncan Blackie: The United Nations and the politics of imperialism ★ Brian Manning: The English Revolution and the transition from feudalism to capitalism ★ Lee Sustar: The roots of multi-racial labour unity in the United States ★ Peter Linebaugh: Days of villainy: a reply to two critics ★ Dave Sherry: Trotsky's last, greatest struggle ★ Peter Morgan: Geronimo and the end of the Indian wars ★ Dave Beecham: Ignazio Silone and *Fontamara* ★ Chris Bambery: Bookwatch: understanding fascism ★

International Socialism 2:62 Spring 1994
Sharon Smith: Mistaken identity—or can identity politics liberate the oppressed? ★ Iain Ferguson: Containing the crisis—crime and the Tories ★ John Newsinger: Orwell and the Spanish Revolution ★ Chris Harman: Change at the first millenium ★ Adrian Budd: Nation and empire—Labour's foreign policy 1945-51 ★ Gareth Jenkins: Novel questions ★ Judy Cox: Blake's revolution ★ Derek Howl: Bookwatch: the Russian Revolution ★

International Socialism 2:61 Winter 1994
Lindsey German: Before the flood? ★ John Molyneux: The 'politically correct' controversy ★ David McNally: E P Thompson—class struggle and historical materialism ★ Charlie Hore: Jazz—a people's music ★ Donny Gluckstein: Revolution and the challenge of labour ★ Charlie Kimber: Bookwatch: the Labour Party in decline ★

International Socialism 2:59 Summer 1993
Ann Rogers: Back to the workhouse ★ Kevin Corr and Andy Brown: The labour aristocracy and the roots of reformism ★ Brian Manning: God, Hill and Marx ★ Henry Maitles: Cutting the wire: a criticial appraisal of Primo Levi ★ Hazel Croft: Bookwatch: women and work ★

International Socialism 2:58 Spring 1993
Chris Harman: Where is capitalism going? (part one) ★ Ruth Brown and Peter Morgan: Politics and the class struggle today: a roundtable discussion ★ Richard Greeman: The return of Comrade Tulayev: Victor Serge and the tragic vision of Stalinism ★ Norah Carlin: A new English revolution ★ John Charlton: Building a new world ★ Colin Barker: A reply to Dave McNally ★

International Socialism 2:56 Autumn 1992
Chris Harman: The Return of the National Question ★ Dave Treece: Why the Earth Summit failed ★ Mike Gonzalez: Can Castro survive? ★ Lee Humber and John Rees: The good old cause—an interview with Christopher Hill ★ Ernest Mandel: The Impasse of Schematic Dogmatism ★

International Socialism 2:55 Summer 1992
Alex Callinicos: Race and class ★ Lee Sustar: Racism and class struggle in the American Civil War era ★ Lindsey German and Peter Morgan: Prospects for socialists—an interview with Tony Cliff ★ Robert Service: Did Lenin lead to Stalin? ★ Samuel Farber: In defence of democratic revolutionary socialism ★ David Finkel: Defending 'October' or sectarian dogmatism? ★ Robin Blackburn: Reply to John Rees ★ John Rees: Dedicated followers of fashion ★ Colin Barker: In praise of custom ★ Sheila McGregor: Revolutionary witness ★

International Socialism 2:51 Summer 1991
Chris Harman: The state and capitalism today ★ Alex Callinicos: The end of nationalism? ★ Sharon Smith: Feminists for a strong state? ★ Colin Sparks and Sue Cockerill: Goodbye to the Swedish miracle ★ Simon Phillips: The South African Communist Party and the South African working class ★ John Brown: Class conflict and the crisis of feudalism ★

International Socialism 2:49 Winter 1990
Chris Bambery: The decline of the Western Communist Parties ★ Ernest Mandel: A theory which has not withstood the test of time ★ Chris Harman: Criticism which does not withstand the test of logic ★ Derek Howl: The law of value In the USSR ★ Terry Eagleton: Shakespeare and the class struggle ★ Lionel Sims: Rape and pre-state societies ★ Sheila McGregor: A reply to Lionel Sims ★

International Socialism 2:48 Autumn 1990
Lindsey German: The last days of Thatcher ★ John Rees: The new imperialism ★ Neil Davidson and Donny Gluckstein: Nationalism and the class struggle in Scotland ★ Paul McGarr: Order out of chaos ★

International Socialism 2:44 Autumn 1989
Charlie Hore: China: Tiananmen Square and after ★ Sue Clegg: Thatcher and the welfare state ★ John Molyneux: *Animal Farm* revisited ★ David Finkel: After Arias, is the revolution over? ★ John Rose: Jews in Poland ★

International Socialism 2:41 Winter 1988
Polish socialists speak out: Solidarity at the Crossroads ★ Mike Haynes: Nightmares of the market ★ Jack Robertson: Socialists and the unions ★ Andy Strouthous: Are the unions in decline? ★ Richard Bradbury: What is Post-Structuralism? ★ Colin Sparks: George Bernard Shaw ★